Lecture Notes in Computer Science 15181

Founding Editors

Gerhard Goos
Juris Hartmanis

Editorial Board Members

Elisa Bertino, *Purdue University, West Lafayette, IN, USA*
Wen Gao, *Peking University, Beijing, China*
Bernhard Steffen , *TU Dortmund University, Dortmund, Germany*
Moti Yung , *Columbia University, New York, NY, USA*

The series Lecture Notes in Computer Science (LNCS), including its subseries Lecture Notes in Artificial Intelligence (LNAI) and Lecture Notes in Bioinformatics (LNBI), has established itself as a medium for the publication of new developments in computer science and information technology research, teaching, and education.

LNCS enjoys close cooperation with the computer science R & D community, the series counts many renowned academics among its volume editors and paper authors, and collaborates with prestigious societies. Its mission is to serve this international community by providing an invaluable service, mainly focused on the publication of conference and workshop proceedings and postproceedings. LNCS commenced publication in 1973.

Jia Wu · Wenjian Qin · Chao Li · Boklye Kim
Editors

Computational Mathematics Modeling in Cancer Analysis

Third International Workshop, CMMCA 2024
Marrakesh, Morocco, October 6, 2024
Proceedings

 Springer

Editors
Jia Wu
The University of Texas MD Anderson
Cancer Center
Houston, TX, USA

Wenjian Qin
Shenzhen Institute of Advanced Technology,
Chinese Academy of Sciences
Shenzhen, China

Chao Li
University of Cambridge
Cambridge, UK

Boklye Kim
National Cancer Institute
Bethesda, MD, USA

ISSN 0302-9743 ISSN 1611-3349 (electronic)
Lecture Notes in Computer Science
ISBN 978-3-031-73359-8 ISBN 978-3-031-73360-4 (eBook)
https://doi.org/10.1007/978-3-031-73360-4

© The Editor(s) (if applicable) and The Author(s), under exclusive license
to Springer Nature Switzerland AG 2025

This work is subject to copyright. All rights are solely and exclusively licensed by the Publisher, whether
the whole or part of the material is concerned, specifically the rights of translation, reprinting, reuse of
illustrations, recitation, broadcasting, reproduction on microfilms or in any other physical way, and transmission
or information storage and retrieval, electronic adaptation, computer software, or by similar or dissimilar
methodology now known or hereafter developed.
The use of general descriptive names, registered names, trademarks, service marks, etc. in this publication
does not imply, even in the absence of a specific statement, that such names are exempt from the relevant
protective laws and regulations and therefore free for general use.
The publisher, the authors and the editors are safe to assume that the advice and information in this book
are believed to be true and accurate at the date of publication. Neither the publisher nor the authors or the
editors give a warranty, expressed or implied, with respect to the material contained herein or for any errors
or omissions that may have been made. The publisher remains neutral with regard to jurisdictional claims in
published maps and institutional affiliations.

This Springer imprint is published by the registered company Springer Nature Switzerland AG
The registered company address is: Gewerbestrasse 11, 6330 Cham, Switzerland

If disposing of this product, please recycle the paper.

Preface

The 3rd Workshop on Computational Mathematics Modeling in Cancer Analysis (CMMCA 2024) was held in conjunction with the 27th International Conference on Medical Image Computing and Computer Assisted Intervention (MICCAI 2024) on October 6, 2024. We gathered with great anticipation in the captivating setting of Morocco to once again exchange knowledge and insights in this evolving field.

Cancer, with its inherent complexity and variability, often presents challenges in accurate diagnosis and treatment planning. In recent years, innovative mathematical and computational approaches, including the concepts of digital twins and foundation models, have begun to make significant inroads into cancer research. These approaches, grounded in rigorous mathematical principles and biological understanding, enable a deep computational analysis of cancer, linking biological mechanisms with insights drawn from a wide range of data sources, such as imaging, pathology, genomics, and proteomics. By integrating clinical data with advanced algorithms in artificial intelligence, these computational methods offer high interpretability and have shown strong potential for practical clinical applications.

CMMCA serves as a platform for collaboration among professionals in mathematics, engineering, computer science, and medicine, focusing on innovative mathematical methods for analyzing complex cancer data. The 2024 workshop emphasized exploring new techniques to tackle current challenges in both theoretical and practical aspects of cancer data analysis. All submissions were subjected to a strict double-blind peer review, evaluated by at least two committee members based on innovation, technical strength, relevance, significance of findings, and presentation clarity. After a competitive review process, 12 papers were selected from the 14 submissions for presentation and publication in this Springer LNCS volume.

Following this successful event, we wish to express our deepest thanks. We are appreciative of the Program Committee for their commitment to thoroughly reviewing the submissions and offering insightful feedback, to the authors for contributing exceptional work, and to the presenters for their engaging presentations. We also extend our gratitude to all the participants of CMMCA 2024, whose global presence and active involvement greatly enhanced the event.

October 2024

Jia Wu
Wenjian Qin
Chao Li
Boklye Kim

Organization

Organizing Chairs

Jia Wu — University of Texas MD Anderson Cancer Center, USA

Wenjian Qin — Shenzhen Institute of Advanced Technology, Chinese Academy of Sciences, China

Chao Li — University of Cambridge, UK

Boklye Kim — National Cancer Institute, USA

Program Committee

Eman Showkatian — University of Texas MD Anderson Cancer Center, USA

Fangliangzi Meng — Tongji University, China

Hao Chen — University of Birmingham, UK

Hongrun Zhang — University of Cambridge, UK

Hui Xu — University of Texas MD Anderson Cancer Center, USA

Jiahui He — Shenzhen Institute of Advanced Technology, Chinese Academy of Sciences, China

Morteza Salehjahromi — University of Texas MD Anderson Cancer Center, USA

Muhammad Waqas — University of Texas MD Anderson Cancer Center, USA

Ruodan Yan — University of Cambridge, UK

Sheeba Sujit — University of Texas MD Anderson Cancer Center, USA

Tian Li — Hong Kong Polytechnic University, China

Wei Zhao — Beihang University, China

Wentao Li — University of Texas MD Anderson Cancer Center, USA

Xiaofei Wang — University of Cambridge, UK

Yaolei Qi — Southeast University, China

Yifan Li — University of Bath, UK

Yupei Zhang — University of Hong Kong, China

Zhenhui Dai   Second Affiliated Hospital, Guangzhou
                             University of Chinese Medicine, China
Zhuohe Liu   University of Texas MD Anderson Cancer Center,
                             USA

Contents

Unified Modeling Enhanced Multimodal Learning for Precision Neuro-Oncology

Huahui Yi[1], Xiaofei Wang[2], Kang Li[1], and Chao Li[2,3,4,5(✉)]

[1] West China Biomedical Big Data Center, West China Hospital, Sichuan University, Chengdu, China

[2] Department of Clinical Neurosciences, University of Cambridge, Cambridge, UK
cl647@cam.ac.uk

[3] Sichuan University Pittsburgh Institute, Chengdu, China

[4] Shanghai AI-Lab, Shanghai, China

[5] School of Medicine, Science and Engineering, University of Dundee, Dundee, UK

Abstract. Multimodal learning, integrating histology images and genomics, promises to enhance precision oncology with comprehensive views at microscopic and molecular levels. However, existing methods may not sufficiently model the shared or complementary information for more effective integration. In this study, we introduce a Unified Modeling Enhanced Multimodal Learning (UMEML) framework that employs a hierarchical attention structure to effectively leverage shared and complementary features of both modalities of histology and genomics. Specifically, to mitigate unimodal bias from modality imbalance, we utilize a query-based cross-attention mechanism for prototype clustering in the pathology encoder. Our prototype assignment and modularity strategy are designed to align shared features and minimizes modality gaps. An additional registration mechanism with learnable tokens is introduced to enhance cross-modal feature integration and robustness in multimodal unified modeling. Our experiments demonstrate that our method surpasses previous state-of-the-art approaches in glioma diagnosis and prognosis tasks, underscoring its superiority in precision neuro-Oncology.

Keywords: Multimodal learning · Glioma · Multimodal classification · Survival prediction

1 Introduction

Multimodal learning [12] refers to the methods of integrating different types of data (e.g., images, genomics) that provides comprehensive information, promising to discover robust feature representations for disease characterization [7]. Integrating multimodal data is particularly relevant for characterizing cancer, a complex disease with remarkable heterogeneity. There is a pressing need to develop multimodal learning approaches for precision oncology [1, 21, 22].

Histopathology is the gold standard in diagnosing cancer. The microscopic morphology observed from tissue sections provides crucial information on tumor

---

Code will be available at: https://github.com/xxx/xxx.

© The Author(s), under exclusive license to Springer Nature Switzerland AG 2025
J. Wu et al. (Eds.): CMMCA 2024, LNCS 15181, pp. 1–10, 2025.
https://doi.org/10.1007/978-3-031-73360-4_1

structure and tissue compositions. Meanwhile, high-throughput sequencing has dramatically accelerated cancer discovery with in-depth genomics profiling, offering opportunities for understanding the molecular underpinnings of cancer. Integrating histopathology with genomics [20] allows for a more holistic approach to study cancer at microscopic and molecular levels. Various computational approaches have been proposed to integrate genomics with histopathology features extracted from histology whole slide images (WSIs) [2,4,14]. For instance, Mobadersany et al. [14] propose to integrate features using vector concatenation, while Chen et al. [2,4] employ Kronecker Product to fuse features. Despite simplicity and efficiency, these methods may ignore the potential correlations and interactions between modalities. Therefore, they cannot fully leverage multimodal information to benefit from robust feature discovery.

To model cross-modal interaction, Chen et al. [3] introduce Genomic-Guided Co-Attention (GCA), using genomics as guidance to identify informative WSIs instances for integration. Zhou et al. [24] propose a Cross-Modal Translation and Alignment framework to transfer and integrate complementary information between modalities. Despite the success, solely relying on either shared or complementary information cannot effectively model complex biological systems for understanding cancer. Effective models remain lacking in utilizing both shared and complementary information in multimodalities. Further, due to the significant tumor heterogeneity and differences in acquisition, histopathology and genomics data present marked noise and modality gaps, challenging effective integration.

To address these challenges, we propose a multimodal learning framework, namely Unified Modeling Enhanced Multimodal Learning (UMEML), to effectively uncover the shared and complementary features from multimodalities and integrate them for precision oncology. Our framework is a hierarchical attention structure comprising two unimodal encoders within each modality and a unified multimodal decoder designed to decode and model the complex relations across modalities. WSI patches typically have much larger quantities than genomics data, causing unimodal bias [23]. To mitigate this challenge, we employ a query-based cross-attention mechanism in the pathology encoder, clustering patch instances into prototypes while concurrently reducing the impact of patch noise. To effectively align shared features from multimodalities while minimizing the modality gap, we design a prototype assignment and modularity strategy. To reduce cross-modal noise and facilitate robust multimodal modeling, a registration mechanism inspired by [5] is introduced, i.e., additional learnable tokens are added between multimodal prototypes, enhancing the learning process for cross-modal feature integration. Our contribution is fourfold:

- We propose the UMEML framework with a hierarchical attention structure. As far as we know, this is the first model to leverage the shared and complementary information between pathology and genomic modalities.
- We employ a prototype query-based cross-attention mechanism in the pathology encoder to mitigate the unimodal bias and reduce patch noise.
- We introduce prototype assignment and modularity strategy to effectively bridge the representation spaces and align shared features.

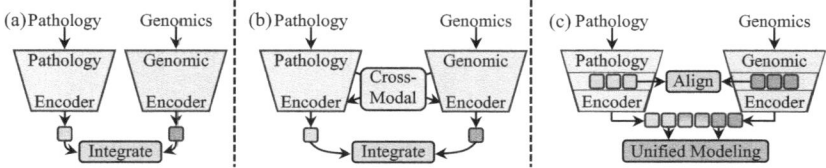

Fig. 1. Illustration of multimodal fusion methods.

- We introduce the registration mechanism to mitigate the noise between multimodalities, enhancing unified modeling for feature integration.

We perform comprehensive experiments on three tasks of glioma grading, classification, and survival prediction. Results show that our model consistently outperforms other state-of-the-art methods, promising to promote precision neuro-oncology.

2 Methodology

2.1 Problem Formulation

The primary goal of multimodal learning is to create a joint representation space that integrates information from multiple communicative modalities. For given pathology and genomic pair (p, g) and label y, where $p \in \mathcal{P}$ in pathology modality, $g \in \mathcal{G}$ in genomics and $y \in \mathcal{Y}$. We denote f_m as a deep network that maps the input in $\mathcal{M}$ modality to latent space, and features across modalities are integrated and passed to a head h. Training is done by minimizing the loss:

$$\mathcal{L}_{\text{multi}} = \mathcal{L}(h(f_p(p) \bigoplus f_g(g)), y) \tag{1}$$

where $\bigoplus$ denotes a fusion operation. Figure 1(a) directly adopts a straightforward fusion of pathology and genomic features (e.g., add, concatenation, Kronecker Product), ignoring the potential correlations and interactions between modalities. As shown in Fig. 1(b), the cross-modal relationship can be decomposed into shared and complementary information. Although studies utilized **either** information [3, 24], we contend that, due to the complexity of cancer, it is crucial to employ **both** information simultaneously. To enhance our understanding of cancer, we propose a novel approach characterized by unified modeling, as illustrated in Fig. 1(c). Specifically, the method employs a hierarchical attention structure and an alignment module to capture shared and unique features, facilitating their unified modeling.

2.2 Overall Structure

Our approach is a hierarchical attention structure, as shown in Fig. 2, beginning with two independent unimodal attention encoders, Pathology Encoder and Genomic Encoder, which model single modality, followed by a unified multimodal attention decoder that models cross-modal relationships.

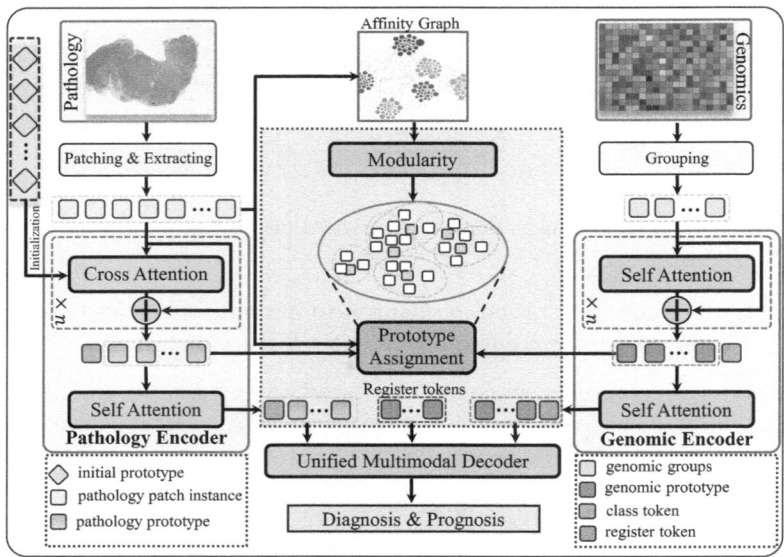

Fig. 2. The proposed UMEML framework. Histopathology-genomic pairs through two unimodal encoders to derive prototypes. The Assignment and Modularity Module refines prototypes using an Affinity Graph, concatenates them with noise-mitigating registers, and inputs them into a Unified Multimodal Decoder for unified representation modeling in downstream tasks.

Pathology Encoder. For the given histopathology patch instance set $P = \{p_1, p_2, \cdots, p_M\} \in \mathbb{R}^{M \times d}$, we define a set of learnable initial prototypes that are iteratively updated through learning the affinity graph among patch instances. Additionally, given that the number of prototypes K is much smaller than M, and approximately equal to N, employing cross-attention to aggregate instances into K prototypes using initial prototypes as *query* effectively mitigates unimodal bias. Specifically, we first apply cross-attention, using the initial prototypes as *query* and the instance representations as *key* and *value*. Let $C^l \in \mathbb{R}^{K \times d}$ denote k prototypes after l-th update and $P \in \mathbb{R}^{M \times d}$ denote M instance representations from a WSI, the cross attention can be formulated as

$$\bar{C}^l = \text{Softmax}(\frac{C^{l-1}W_q(PW_k)^T}{\sqrt{d}})(XW_v), \quad C^l = C^{l-1} + \bar{C}^l, \quad (2)$$

where $W_q, W_k, W_v \in \mathbb{R}^{d \times d}$ are learnable linear projections. The cross-attention updates prototypes adaptively with the patch-level representations, which makes it possible to generate high-semantic centers adaptively for different WSIs.

Upon completing cross-attention processes, a learnable class token of pathology is concatenated to the front of C^l, forming $\hat{C}^l$ to be fed into a self-attention modeling the interconnection between prototypes. $\hat{C}^l$ is expressed as

$$\hat{C}^l = [T_{CLS}, C^l]. \quad (3)$$

The self-attention updates each prototype in relation to others, thereby enhancing its awareness of other prototypes.

Genomic Encoder. For the given Genomics $G = \{g_1, g_2, \cdots, g_N\} \in \mathbb{R}^{N \times d}$, we posit that each gene group, post-grouping, serves as a natural prototype, and thus, we directly feed them into multiple self-attention modules to model the interrelations among gene groups. Similarly to Pathology Encoder, we introduce a new learnable gene class token. This class token is concatenated with the previous output P^l to form $\hat{P}^l$ fed into another self-attention module.

Unified Multimodal Decoder. Composed of n self-attention layers. Through unified modeling, the encoder learns the shared and complementary information, thereby enhancing and augmenting the feature integration for downstream tasks.

2.3   Prototype Assignment and Modularity

Prototype Assignment. For given pathology prototypes $C \in \mathbb{R}^{K \times d}$, genomic prototypes $G \in \mathbb{R}^{N \times d}$, and histopathology patch instances $P \in \mathbb{R}^{M \times d}$, we calculate the respective prototype assignment matrices $S^p \in \mathbb{R}^{K \times M}$ for C and P, $S^g \in \mathbb{R}^{N \times M}$ for G and P. Taking S^p as an example, the equation is as follows:

$$S^p = \max(0, \cos < C, P >), \tag{4}$$

Thereby, we allocate a certain number of patch instances to each prototype and segment a WSI into K and N regions based on pathology and genomics prototypes. Each region, defined by a unique concept, contains associated instances.

Modularity. We employ modularity to optimize the assignment between prototypes and patches, a method commonly used in community detection [10, 15, 16]. Specifically, we first construct a fully connected, undirected affinity graph $A \in \mathbb{R}^{M \times M}$ for instances from a WSI, treated as vertices. The expression for A is:

$$A = \max(0, \cos < P, P >), \tag{5}$$

We then compute a weight matrix W to estimate the intensity of assigning them to the same concept by

$$W = A - \frac{dd^{\mathrm{T}}}{2e}, \tag{6}$$

where degree vector $d \in \mathbb{R}^M$ denotes the number of connected edges in its affinity A, and $e \in \mathbb{R}$ signifies the total edge number. By considering both prototype assignment S and affinity matrix A, the modularity loss is formulated as:

$$\mathcal{L}_{\mathrm{modularity}} = -\frac{1}{2e}(\alpha \mathrm{Tr}(W(S^{p^T}S^p)) + \beta \mathrm{Tr}W(S^{g^T}S^g))), \tag{7}$$

Here, α and β are hyperparameters that modulate the impacts of various components within the modularity loss function, respectively. This loss refines prototype similarity for various instance pairs by assessing their likelihood of sharing a concept, thereby updating the prototype locations in the representation space while considering instance-specific locality and connectivity. Then the total loss is calculated as

$$\mathcal{L}_{\mathrm{total}} = \mathcal{L}_{\mathrm{objective}} + \gamma \mathcal{L}_{\mathrm{modularity}}, \tag{8}$$

Here, γ represents a positive hyperparameter that balances the impact of the modularity loss function on the overall model performance. For objective part, We use the cross-entropy loss for grading and classification and negative log-likelihood survival loss [3] for survival prediction.

2.4   Registration Mechanism

The registration mechanism [5] adds a set of additional learnable tokens, called register tokens, between pathology and genomic prototypes. By learning additional relationships during the attention process, this mechanism helps reduce the disturbances caused by outliers and mismatches. Concretely, for the given pathology prototypes $\hat{C}^{l+1} \in \mathbb{R}^{(K+1) \times d}$, genomic prototypes $\hat{G}^{l+1} \in \mathbb{R}^{(N+1) \times d}$, we introduce additional learnable register tokens $R \in \mathbb{R}^{I \times d}$. These elements are then concatenated,

$$\hat{U} = [\hat{C}^{l+1}, R, \hat{G}^{l+1}]. \tag{9}$$

The concatenated output $\hat{U}$ is fed into the unified multimodal decoder.

3   Experiments

3.1   Datasets and Experiments Setting

Dataset. We evaluate our model on diagnosis (grading, classification) and prognosis (survival prediction) using the TCGA GBM-LGG dataset [6], comprising 939 patient samples and 1831 WSIs after excluding low-quality WSIs or those missing labels following prior work [13,20]. We crop each WSI into non-overlapping $224 \, \text{px} \times 224 \, \text{px}$ patches at $0.5 \, \mu\text{m} \, \text{px}^{-1}$. CLIP ViT-B/16 [18] is used to extract 512-dimensional features from histopathology patches, and the top-K genes with the highest expression variance are selected and categorized into N uniform groups for genomic profile input.

Experiments Setting. All experiments were conducted on a single NVIDIA RTX 3090 GPU using the PyTorch library [17] within the Python environment, with a batch size 1. To ensure representative experimental results, we employ a 5-fold cross-validation approach, using the corresponding seed for each fold during training (e.g., fold = 1, seed = 1). Experiments used SGD with a $1e-5$ weight decay, training the model for ten epochs with a $1e-3$ learning rate for diagnosis and five epochs with a $2e-4$ learning rate for prognosis. Results were averaged over five folds, considering each fold's final epoch.

3.2   Performance Evaluation

We implemented and compared state-of-the-art methods and baselines, covering single-modal (SNN [9], AttMIL [8], TransMIL [19]) and multimodal learning (Add, Concat, Kronecker Product, MCAT [3], HFBSurv [11], CMAT [24]) learning approaches. Table 1 shows the results of all methods.

Table 1. The performance of different approaches on three common medical tasks on TCGA GBM-LGG dataset. "P." indicates whether pathological images are used and "G." indicates whether genomic profiles are used. The best and second best results are highlighted in red and blue, respectively.

Methods	Modality		Grading		Classification		Survival
	P.	G.	Acc	AUC	Acc	AUC	C-Index
SNN [9]		✓	$0.7054^{\pm\ 0.0187}$	$0.8438^{\pm\ 0.0205}$	$0.5956^{\pm\ 0.0345}$	$0.8476^{\pm\ 0.0246}$	$0.7746^{\pm\ 0.0413}$
AttMIL [8]	✓		$0.6392^{\pm\ 0.0229}$	$0.8118^{\pm\ 0.0167}$	$0.5482^{\pm\ 0.0315}$	$0.7998^{\pm\ 0.0274}$	$0.7560^{\pm\ 0.0434}$
TransMIL [19]	✓		$0.5852^{\pm\ 0.0206}$	$0.7420^{\pm\ 0.0126}$	$0.4584^{\pm\ 0.0233}$	$0.7068^{\pm\ 0.0210}$	$0.7110^{\pm\ 0.0361}$
Add	✓	✓	$0.6924^{\pm\ 0.0415}$	$0.8598^{\pm\ 0.0161}$	$0.6072^{\pm\ 0.0191}$	$0.8710^{\pm\ 0.0275}$	$0.7960^{\pm\ 0.0514}$
Concat	✓	✓	$0.7264^{\pm\ 0.0406}$	$0.8864^{\pm\ 0.0164}$	$0.6740^{\pm\ 0.0160}$	$0.9218^{\pm\ 0.0100}$	$0.8300^{\pm\ 0.0324}$
Kronecker	✓	✓	$0.7312^{\pm\ 0.0401}$	$0.8830^{\pm\ 0.0175}$	$0.6596^{\pm\ 0.0353}$	$0.9096^{\pm\ 0.0181}$	$0.8224^{\pm\ 0.0291}$
MCAT [3]	✓	✓	$0.7376^{\pm\ 0.0307}$	$0.9092^{\pm\ 0.0164}$	$0.6932^{\pm\ 0.0480}$	$0.9470^{\pm\ 0.0113}$	$0.8352^{\pm\ 0.0227}$
HFBSurv [11]	✓	✓	$0.6906^{\pm\ 0.0193}$	$0.8506^{\pm\ 0.0142}$	$0.6600^{\pm\ 0.0239}$	$0.8506^{\pm\ 0.0244}$	$0.8202^{\pm\ 0.0307}$
CMAT [24]	✓	✓	$0.7228^{\pm\ 0.0226}$	$0.9020^{\pm\ 0.0175}$	$0.7186^{\pm\ 0.0289}$	$0.9538^{\pm\ 0.0070}$	$0.8286^{\pm\ 0.0383}$
(Ours)	✓	✓	$0.7756^{\pm\ 0.0178}$	$0.9212^{\pm\ 0.0147}$	$0.7514^{\pm\ 0.0380}$	$0.9594^{\pm\ 0.0069}$	$0.8396^{\pm\ 0.0292}$

Compared with Single-modal Models. As shown in Table 1, our proposed method consistently outperforms other models in all tasks. For grading, our model achieves an accuracy of 77.56% and an AUC of 92.12%, surpassing the best single-modal method by 7.02% and an AUC of 7.74%, respectively. For classification, it attains an accuracy of 75.14% and an AUC of 95.94%, exceeding the best single-modal method by 15.58% and 11.18%, respectively. For survival prediction, our model achieves a c-index of 83.96%, an improvement of 6.50% over the top single-modal method. These results underscore the benefit of multimodal learning, where integrating multimodalities may enhance model performance.

Compared with Multimodal Models. For grading, Table 1 (columns 4 and 5) demonstrates that our method outperforms the state-of-the-art multimodal method, MCAT, surpassing the accuracy by 3.80% and AUC by 1.20%. For classification, our approach surpasses the leading method, CMAT (columns 6 and 7), with an increase of 3.28% in accuracy and 0.56% in AUC. Furthermore, for survival prediction, a 0.44% improvement in the c-index over MCAT is shown in column 8. These results suggest our model's advantages of leveraging shared and complementary information. Our method also significantly outperforms other comparison multimodal methods, including Add, Concat, Kronecker Product, and HFBSurv [11], demonstrating consistently superior performance.

3.3   Ablation Studies

We remove or replace the key components to investigate their impact on model performance in (Table 2). After removing the modularity loss, the accuracy for grading decreases by 1.00% and the AUC by −0.04%. For classification, the accuracy drops by 1.40% and the AUC by 0.16%. For survival prediction, the c-index reduces by 0.28%. These results imply that minimizing the modality gap

Table 2. The ablation study of three key components: 1) Omitting the Modularity Loss; 2) Replacing the Unified Multimodal Decoder (UMD) with a Bi-fusion module; 3) Excluding the using of registers in the UMD.

Components	Grading		Classification		Survival
	Acc	AUC	Acc	AUC	C-Index
w/o Modularity	$0.7656^{\pm\ 0.0175}$	$0.9216^{\pm\ 0.0142}$	$0.7374^{\pm\ 0.0305}$	$0.9578^{\pm\ 0.0072}$	$0.8368^{\pm\ 0.0252}$
w/o UMD	$0.7612^{\pm\ 0.0216}$	$0.9192^{\pm\ 0.0187}$	$0.7266^{\pm\ 0.0315}$	$0.9538^{\pm\ 0.0074}$	$0.8376^{\pm\ 0.0226}$
w/o Registers	$0.7620^{\pm\ 0.0195}$	$0.9168^{\pm\ 0.0212}$	$0.7266^{\pm\ 0.0216}$	$0.9546^{\pm\ 0.0061}$	$0.8368^{\pm\ 0.0288}$
Ours (All)	$0.7756^{\pm\ 0.0178}$	$0.9212^{\pm\ 0.0147}$	$0.7514^{\pm\ 0.0380}$	$0.9594^{\pm\ 0.0069}$	$0.8396^{\pm\ 0.0292}$

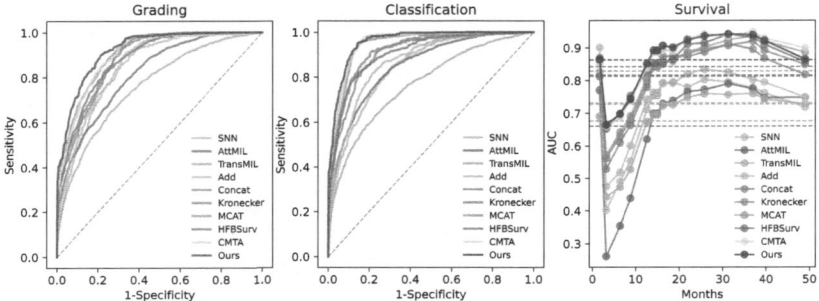

Fig. 3. Compare our method's ROC curves for glioma grading and classification and time-dependent AUC curves for survival prediction against other methods.

benefits unified multimodal modeling. When the Unified Multimodal Decoder (UMD) is replaced by Bi-fusion, a widely-used cross-attention-based multimodal integration module, the accuracy for grading decreases by 1.44% and the AUC by 0.20%. For classification, the accuracy drops by 2.48% and the AUC by 0.56%. For survival prediction, the c-index reduces by 0.20%. These findings imply that compared to Bi-fusion, UMD can model more complex relationships and suit multimodal cancer modeling. After removing the register, we observe a decrease in accuracy by 1.36% and AUC by 0.44% for grading, a decrease in accuracy by 2.48% and AUC by 0.48% for classification, and a decrease in the c-index by 0.28% for survival prediction. These results imply that the register contributes to the UMD's ability to model more robust multimodal relationships.

Additionally, we have illustrated both ROC curves (glioma grading and classification) and time-dependent AUC curves (survival prediction) in Fig. 3 further to demonstrate the superiority and robustness of our method.

4   Conclusion

This paper proposes a unified modeling approach with a hierarchical attention structure that effectively leverages both shared and complementary information from multimodal learning. To avoid unimodal bias, we address the imbalance between pathology patches and genomics groups through prototype-based cross-attention. We align these modalities using prototype assignment and modularity to reduce modeling errors arising from the modality gap. This Unified Multimodal Decoder is supplemented by the registration mechanism to reduce noises between modalities. The results show that our model achieves state-of-the-art performance. Given the cost of acquiring multimodal data, future research will address missing modalities in multimodal learning.

References

1. Boehm, K.M., Khosravi, P., Vanguri, R., Gao, J., Shah, S.P.: Harnessing multimodal data integration to advance precision oncology. Nat. Rev. Cancer **22**(2), 114–126 (2022)
2. Chen, R.J., et al.: Pathomic fusion: an integrated framework for fusing histopathology and genomic features for cancer diagnosis and prognosis. IEEE Trans. Med. Imaging **41**(4), 757–770 (2020)
3. Chen, R.J., et al.: Multimodal co-attention transformer for survival prediction in gigapixel whole slide images. In: Proceedings of the IEEE/CVF International Conference on Computer Vision, pp. 4015–4025 (2021)
4. Chen, R.J., et al.: Pan-cancer integrative histology-genomic analysis via multimodal deep learning. Cancer Cell **40**(8), 865–878 (2022)
5. Darcet, T., Oquab, M., Mairal, J., Bojanowski, P.: Vision transformers need registers. arXiv preprint arXiv:2309.16588 (2023)
6. https://portal.gdc.cancer.gov/
7. Huang, Y., Du, C., Xue, Z., Chen, X., Zhao, H., Huang, L.: What makes multimodal learning better than single (provably). Adv. Neural. Inf. Process. Syst. **34**, 10944–10956 (2021)
8. Ilse, M., Tomczak, J., Welling, M.: Attention-based deep multiple instance learning. In: International Conference on Machine Learning, pp. 2127–2136. PMLR (2018)
9. Klambauer, G., Unterthiner, T., Mayr, A., Hochreiter, S.: Self-normalizing neural networks. In: Advances in Neural Information Processing Systems, vol. 30 (2017)
10. Li, K., et al.: ACSeg: adaptive conceptualization for unsupervised semantic segmentation. In: Proceedings of the IEEE/CVF Conference on Computer Vision and Pattern Recognition, pp. 7162–7172 (2023)
11. Li, R., Wu, X., Li, A., Wang, M.: HFBSurv: hierarchical multimodal fusion with factorized bilinear models for cancer survival prediction. Bioinformatics **38**(9), 2587–2594 (2022)
12. Liang, P.P., Zadeh, A., Morency, L.P.: Foundations and recent trends in multimodal machine learning: Principles, challenges, and open questions. arXiv preprint arXiv:2209.03430 (2022)
13. Lu, M.Y., Williamson, D.F., Chen, T.Y., Chen, R.J., Barbieri, M., Mahmood, F.: Data-efficient and weakly supervised computational pathology on whole-slide images. Nat. Biom. Eng. **5**(6), 555–570 (2021)
14. Mobadersany, P., et al.: Predicting cancer outcomes from histology and genomics using convolutional networks. Proc. Nat. Acad. Sci. **115**(13), E2970–E2979 (2018)
15. Newman, M.E.: Modularity and community structure in networks. Proc. Nat. Acad. Sci. **103**(23), 8577–8582 (2006)

16. Newman, M.E., Girvan, M.: Finding and evaluating community structure in networks. Phys. Rev. E **69**(2), 026113 (2004)
17. Paszke, A., et al.: PyTorch: an imperative style, high-performance deep learning library. In: Advances in Neural Information Processing Systems, vol. 32 (2019)
18. Radford, A., et al.: Learning transferable visual models from natural language supervision. In: International Conference on Machine Learning, pp. 8748–8763. PMLR (2021)
19. Shao, Z., et al.: TransMIL: transformer based correlated multiple instance learning for whole slide image classification. Adv. Neural. Inf. Process. Syst. **34**, 2136–2147 (2021)
20. Wang, X., Price, S., Li, C.: Multi-task learning of histology and molecular markers for classifying diffuse glioma. arXiv preprint arXiv:2303.14845 (2023)
21. Wei, Y., et al.: Multi-modal learning for predicting the genotype of glioma. IEEE Trans. Med. Imaging **42**, 3167–3178 (2023)
22. Wei, Y., Li, C., Chen, X., Schönlieb, C.B., Price, S.J.: Collaborative learning of images and geometrics for predicting isocitrate dehydrogenase status of glioma. In: 2022 IEEE 19th International Symposium on Biomedical Imaging (ISBI), pp. 1–4. IEEE (2022)
23. Zhang, Y., Latham, P.E., Saxe, A.: A theory of unimodal bias in multimodal learning. arXiv preprint arXiv:2312.00935 (2023)
24. Zhou, F., Chen, H.: Cross-modal translation and alignment for survival analysis. In: Proceedings of the IEEE/CVF International Conference on Computer Vision, pp. 21485–21494 (2023)

A Reference-Based Approach for Tumor Size Estimation in Monocular Laparoscopic Videos

Seyed Amir Mousavi[1,2(✉)], Francesca Tozzi[3,5], Homin Park[1,2],
Esla Timothy Anzaku[1,2], Matthias Van Liefferinge[5], Nikdokht Rashidian[4,5],
Wouter Willaert[3,5], and Wesley De Neve[1,2]

[1] IDLab, ELIS, Ghent University, Ghent, Belgium
{seyedamir.mousavi,homin.park,eslatimothy.anzaku,
wesley.deneve}@ghent.ac.kr
[2] Center for Biosystems and Biotech Data Science, Ghent University Global Campus,
Incheon, Korea
[3] Department of GI Surgery, Ghent University Hospital, Ghent, Belgium
[4] Department of HPB Surgery and Liver Transplantation, Ghent University Hospital,
Ghent, Belgium
[5] Department of Human Structure and Repair, Ghent University, Ghent, Belgium
{francesca.tozzi,matthias.vanliefferinge,nikdokht.rashidian,
wouter.willaert}@ugent.be

Abstract. Laparoscopic exploration of the abdominal cavity is routinely performed for the diagnosis, assessment, and staging of peritoneal metastasis (PM). Accurately measuring tumor size during this procedure is crucial for prognosis and treatment planning. As conventional approaches for tumor size measurement rely on subjective manual assessments during or after surgery, they stand to benefit from computer assistance. This study proposes a new method for measuring tumor size in laparoscopic monocular videos. Specifically, we introduce a novel mathematical equation that connects the intrinsic parameters of a monocular camera, the surface area of target and reference objects, and their distances to the camera. Furthermore, we combine this equation with an object segmentation model (Mask2Former) and a depth estimation model (MiDaS), creating an end-to-end framework that automates tumor size measurement in monocular laparoscopic videos. We evaluate the proposed method using a laparoscopy dataset comprising 18 videos depicting 76 tumor biopsies, with tumor size measured by surgeons who are experts in laparoscopic surgery. When estimating the size of the various tumors in this dataset, we obtain a Mean Absolute Error (MAE) of 2.44 mm ± 0.23 mm, demonstrating that the newly proposed method accurately predicts intraoperative tumor size. Our code and the evaluation dataset are publicly available on https://github.com/amiiiirrrr/TSEMLV.

Keywords: Laparoscopy · Monocular Vision · Tumor Size Estimation

---

S. A. Mousavi and F. Tozzi—These authors have contributed equally to this work.

© The Author(s), under exclusive license to Springer Nature Switzerland AG 2025
J. Wu et al. (Eds.): CMMCA 2024, LNCS 15181, pp. 11–20, 2025.
https://doi.org/10.1007/978-3-031-73360-4_2

1   Introduction

Peritoneal metastasis (PM) consists of the development of malignant tumors within the peritoneal layer of the abdominal cavity. In controlling the spread of cancer in the peritoneum, conventional approaches such as chemotherapy and surgery may prove ineffective. Laparoscopic exploration of the abdominal cavity is considered the gold standard for diagnosing PM and assessing its extension within the abdomen. Accurate evaluation of the extension of PM enables proper treatment planning and follow-up for this oncological condition [2].

The Peritoneal Cancer Index (PCI) assesses tumoral load, allowing a semi-quantitative evaluation of the evolution of PM. PCI is routinely used during laparoscopic exploration [8,11,13]. Additionally, the effectiveness of chemotherapy can be measured by the accurate determination of tumor size during laparoscopic exploration before and after treatment. Inaccurate tumor size estimation could compromise the evaluation of the effectiveness of chemotherapy in targeting PM, potentially leading to an inadequate treatment approach and unnecessary treatments. This might result in an increased risk of side effects with no additional therapeutic benefit. Moreover, due to the absence of a universally accepted method for determining the size of abdominal tumors, and the fact that clinicians are currently compelled to rely on subjective estimations, this approach stands to benefit from automation, for example, through the adoption of modern computer vision techniques. In this paper, we introduce a comprehensive solution to the problem of tumor size measurement, describing an end-to-end method that objectively assesses tumor size in laparoscopic videos that have been obtained from a monocular camera. In particular, our contributions can be summarized as follows:

- We derived a novel mathematical equation that establishes a relationship between the intrinsic parameters of a monocular camera, the surface area of target and reference objects, and their distances to the camera.
- We combined the derived equation with state-of-the-art object segmentation (through Mask2Former [5]) and depth estimation (through MiDaS [4]). This resulted in an end-to-end method that takes laparoscopic videos as input and outputs tumor size measurements, thereby automating the entire process.
- Mask2Former is trained on 30 videos, 2309 frames, annotated by medical experts for 27 abdominal cavity organs, tumors, and surgical instruments.
- The newly introduced approach is validated using a dataset comprising 18 videos depicting 76 biopsies, with a ground truth created by skilled surgeons.

2   Related Work

The authors of [6] introduce a method for computing 3-D affine measurements from a single perspective view using minimal geometric information, such as the vanishing line of a reference plane and the vanishing point for a non-parallel direction. Andalo et al. [3] focus on height measurements in standalone images, employing a vanishing point detector and demonstrating how to estimate the vertical direction and detect the ground plane vanishing line. However, these methods are effective for man-made environments and struggle with scenes lacking parallel lines or lines not aligned with the coordinate system axis. Indeed, in PM, the complex abdominal cavity structure poses challenges for accurate linear segment extraction, making traditional computer vision techniques impractical for estimating vanishing points in medical imagery.

In the evolving field of GastroIntestinal (GI) endoscopy, recent developments in tumor size measurement include a method proposed by Zhou *et al.* that is using Video Capsule Endoscopy (VCE) frames. Their approach, outlined in [17], employs RGB channels and a Support Vector Machine (SVM) to detect and determine polyp sizes. Additionally, in [12], Oka *et al.* introduce a novel lesion size measurement system that combines an inexpensive optical device with a conventional endoscope. This system measures target lesion sizes by displaying a grid scale on endoscopic images, with the grid width adjusting in real-time based on the distance between the endoscope tip and the lesion. [10] presents a novel system for contactless measurement in endoscopy, specifically focusing on wireless capsule endoscopes (WCE). It employs a deep convolutional image registration method combined with a multi-layer feed-forward neural network to accurately measure lesion locations and sizes within the gastrointestinal tract.

Another study by [7] introduces a virtual tape-measure prototype utilizing a laser line to accurately measure polyp sizes during colonoscopies. While the prototype yields highly accurate results, challenges arise from the quality of the projected laser line. Additionally, [14] presents a novel Structured Light (SL) laser probe embedded into a conventional endoscope for one-shot size measurement of polyps during flexible endoscopy of the stomach. The proposed probe significantly reduces errors in polyp size estimation compared to visual inspection. Indeed, lesions can be precisely measured via laser or light projection techniques, whereas the necessity for supplementary instruments to be attached to the endoscope restricts their suitability for specific surgical procedures.

To function effectively, the aforementioned studies require additional devices or specific conditions in a controlled environment and are not open-sourced for reproduction. In contrast, our method is the first to automate tumor size measurement in PM using only a standard monocular camera typically employed in these surgeries. This eliminates the need for extra equipment or special setups suited for the dynamic environment of the abdominal cavity, which features complex anatomical structures, tissue deformation, and variable lighting conditions, making accurate measurements challenging, especially when combined with irregular camera movements.

3   Methodology

As shown in Fig. 1, this paper proposes a novel method to calculate the surface area of a tumor, our target object, based on the known diameter of a Surgical Instrument (SI), our reference object. In more detail, we employed Mask2Former

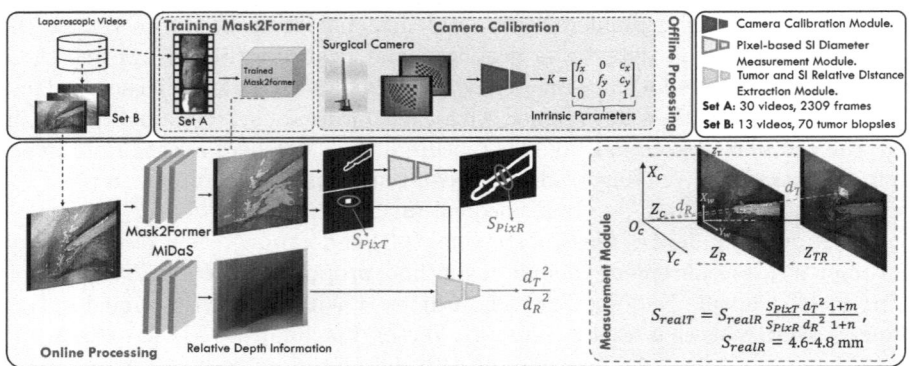

Fig. 1. Overview of the proposed method: Offline processing consists of calibrating the camera to obtain intrinsic parameters and using an annotated Set A to train a segmentation model. Online processing entails the use of a module that computes the relative distance, a module that measures the SI diameter in pixels, and a measurement module that integrates all data to estimate the size of a tumor.

to extract the pixel surface area of the tumor, and then generate a bounding box (S_{PixT}) from the segmentation mask of the tumor that encompasses it. MiDaS is used to determine the relative distance between tumors and the SI. Determining the pixel thickness of the SI (S_{PixR}) in videos is a critical step that is illustrated by the red line in Fig. 1. To do so using OpenCV, the pixels of the SI are first obtained using Mask2Former, and then its contour is generated. Next, the center point of the contour is found. By finding the elongation angle of the SI contour, it is possible to derive a line that passes through the center point of the contour and is perpendicular to the line along the elongation direction of the SI. This line represents the pixel thickness of the SI. In what follows, we establish a relationship between the real-world surfaces of the reference and target objects, their pixel area, and their relative distances to the camera by adopting pinhole camera imaging.

3.1   A Reference-Based Object Size Measurement Model

The authors of [16] introduce a novel method for absolute localization estimation of a target using monocular vision. Specifically, they calculate the absolute distance between the camera and the target by mapping 3-D points in the world to a 2-D image generated through pinhole imaging. The research effort presented in this paper broadens the scope of the method presented in [16], facilitating dimension measurement of the target object using a reference object. To that end, we also rely on pinhole imaging, which maps 3-D objects to a 2-D plane, given its adequacy for measuring objects in world coordinates via camera calibration. We assume the reader has some basic awareness of both pinhole imaging [9] and the method discussed in [16].

Reference Object - As shown in Fig. 2, (X_R, Y_R, Z_R) and (X_{wr}, Y_{wr}, Z_{wr}) are two points on the reference plane that correspond to the camera and world coordinate system, respectively. The world coordinate system is positioned on the surface of the reference object, wherein the optical axis meets the reference object plane [16]. That way, the rotation $R = diag(1, 1, 1)$ and translation $T = (0, 0, Z_R)^T$ matrices are attainable. The conversion of world coordinates to pixel coordinates can be mathematically represented as follows:

$$Z_R \begin{bmatrix} u \\ v \\ 1 \end{bmatrix} = \begin{bmatrix} f_x & 0 & c_x & 0 \\ 0 & f_y & c_y & 0 \\ 0 & 0 & 1 & 0 \end{bmatrix} \begin{bmatrix} R & T \\ O^T & 1 \end{bmatrix} \begin{bmatrix} X_{wr} \\ Y_{wr} \\ Z_{wr} \\ 1 \end{bmatrix} = \begin{bmatrix} f_x & 0 & c_x & c_x Z_R \\ 0 & f_y & c_y & c_y Z_R \\ 0 & 0 & 1 & Z_R \end{bmatrix} \begin{bmatrix} X_{wr} \\ Y_{wr} \\ Z_{wr} \\ 1 \end{bmatrix} \quad (1)$$

Note that f denotes the focal length of the camera and (u, v) represents the pixel coordinate frame. In this paper, m_x and m_y are defined as the number of pixels per unit distance along the x and y axes of the pixel coordinates, respectively. $f_x = f m_x$ and $f_y = f m_y$ denote the focal length of the camera in the x and y directions, respectively, and (c_x, c_y) represents the principal point in the image plane that intersects the optical axis. Figure 2 illustrates that the reference object can be divided into N rectangles along the X_w axis within the scene, creating roughly rectangular pieces. It should also be evident that $Z_w = 0$ for the reference object, and through simplification of Eq. 1, it is feasible to obtain the real surface area S_{realR} of the reference object as follows:

$$\sum_{i=1}^{N} (P_{2y}^i - P_{1y}^i)(P_{1x}^{i+1} - P_{1x}^i) = \frac{Z_R^2}{f_x f_y} \sum_{i=1}^{N} (v_2^i - v_1^i)(u_1^{i+1} - u_1^i) = S_{PixR} \frac{Z_R^2}{f_x f_y} \quad (2)$$

where S_{pixR} is the pixel-wise representation of the area of the reference object on the image plane, and P_{1x}^i and P_{1y}^i represent the coordinates of point P_1^i in the X_w and Y_w directions, respectively, in the world coordinate system. Following this, the absolute distance between the camera and the reference object, $d_R = \|\mathbf{P_{FR}} - \mathbf{O_c}\|$, can be obtained through the establishment of the relationship between a point in the image plane (u_{FR}, v_{FR}), which is the midpoint of the shape of the reference object in the image, and its corresponding point $P_{FR} = (X_{FR}, Y_{FR})$ in the world plane. This can be expressed as follows:

$$d_R = Z_R \sqrt{(X_{FR})^2 + (Y_{FR})^2 + 1} \quad , \quad \begin{bmatrix} X_{FR} \\ Y_{FR} \\ 1 \end{bmatrix} = Z_R \begin{bmatrix} (u_{FR} - c_x)/f_x \\ (v_{FR} - c_y)/f_y \\ 1/Z_R \end{bmatrix} \quad (3)$$

$$S_{realR} = \frac{d_R^2}{1 + e_r} \frac{S_{PixR}}{f_x f_y} \quad , \quad e_r = (\frac{u_{FR} - c_x}{f_x})^2 + (\frac{v_{FR} - c_y}{f_y})^2 \quad (4)$$

Target Object - In what follows, we replicate the above approach for the target object, targeting the derivation of a formula that connects the surface area of

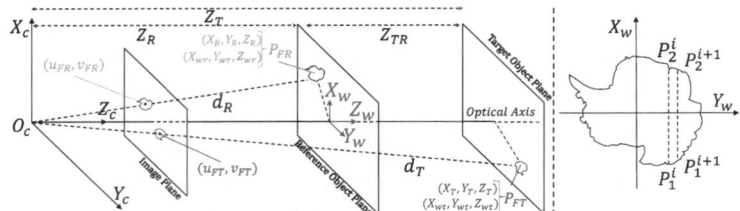

Fig. 2. Geometry for calculating the surface area of the target object from the surface area of the reference object and their respective distances to the projection center.

the target object to the absolute distance d_T between the target object and the camera center. Assume the points (X_T, Y_T, Z_T) and (X_{wt}, Y_{wt}, Z_{wt}) of the target object belong to the camera and world coordinate system, respectively. These points are transformed into pixel coordinates (u, v) using the pinhole camera model as follows:

$$
Z_{\mathrm{T}} \begin{bmatrix} u \\ v \\ 1 \end{bmatrix} = \begin{bmatrix} f_x & 0 & c_x & 0 \\ 0 & f_y & c_y & 0 \\ 0 & 0 & 1 & 0 \end{bmatrix} \begin{bmatrix} X_T \\ Y_T \\ Z_T \\ 1 \end{bmatrix} = \begin{bmatrix} f_x & 0 & c_x & 0 \\ 0 & f_y & c_y & 0 \\ 0 & 0 & 1 & 0 \end{bmatrix} \begin{bmatrix} \mathrm{R} & \mathrm{T} \\ \mathrm{O}^T & 1 \end{bmatrix} \begin{bmatrix} X_{wt} \\ Y_{wt} \\ Z_{wt} \\ 1 \end{bmatrix} \quad (5)
$$

In this context, we maintain $R = diag(1, 1, 1)$ and $T = (0, 0, Z_R)^T$, given that these matrices are exclusively employed for the purpose of converting world coordinates to camera coordinates, and the world coordinate system was previously fixed on the reference object plane. In this case, however, it should be evident that $Z_{wt} = Z_{\mathrm{TR}}$, where Z_{TR} is the distance between the target and reference planes. This is an important difference with the approach followed for the reference object. Consequently, Eq. 5 can be reformulated as follows:

$$
Z_T \begin{bmatrix} u \\ v \\ 1 \end{bmatrix} = \begin{bmatrix} f_x & 0 & c_x & c_x Z_R \\ 0 & f_y & c_y & c_y Z_R \\ 0 & 0 & 1 & Z_R \end{bmatrix} \begin{bmatrix} X_{wt} \\ Y_{wt} \\ Z_{wt} \\ 1 \end{bmatrix} = \begin{bmatrix} f_x & 0 & c_x(Z_{TR} + Z_R) \\ 0 & f_y & c_y(Z_{TR} + Z_R) \\ 0 & 0 & Z_{TR} + Z_R \end{bmatrix} \begin{bmatrix} X_{wt} \\ Y_{wt} \\ 1 \end{bmatrix} \quad (6)
$$

By applying Eq. 2 and Eq. 3 to the target object, we can establish a connection between the distance of the target object to the camera center ($d_T = \|\mathbf{P_{FT}} - \mathbf{O_c}\|$), its actual surface size (S_{realT}), its surface size in pixels (S_{pixT}), and the intrinsic parameters of the camera:

$$
d_T = Z_T \sqrt{(X_{FT})^2 + (Y_{FT})^2 + 1} \quad , \quad \begin{bmatrix} X_{FT} \\ Y_{FT} \\ 1 \end{bmatrix} = Z_T \begin{bmatrix} (u_{FT} - c_x)/f_x \\ (v_{FT} - c_y)/f_y \\ 1/Z_T \end{bmatrix} \quad (7)
$$

$$S_{realT} = \frac{d_T^2}{1 + e_t} \frac{S_{PixT}}{f_x f_y} \quad , \quad e_t = \left(\frac{u_{FT} - c_x}{f_x}\right)^2 + \left(\frac{v_{FT} - c_y}{f_y}\right)^2 \qquad (8)$$

where (u_{FT}, v_{FT}) is a point on the target image plane that represents the center of the shape of the target object in the picture, and $P_{FR} = (X_{FR}, Y_{FR})$ is its equivalent point on the target world plane. Finally, through the integration of Eq. 4 and Eq. 8, we can derive a formula that describes a connection between the real-world surface sizes of the reference and the target objects, alongside their corresponding pixel surfaces and distances to the camera:

$$S_{realT} = S_{realR} \frac{S_{PixT}}{S_{PixR}} \frac{d_T^2}{d_R^2} \frac{1 + e_r}{1 + e_t} \qquad (9)$$

By applying this equation in conjunction with (i) a segmentation model to determine the pixel surface areas of the objects and (ii) a depth estimator model that supplies the relative distances between the SI and the tumor to the camera, we are able to measure the size of a tumor.

4   Experimental Results

To calibrate the surgical camera (5 mm, 30° scopes, Olympus, Hamburg, Germany), multiple checkerboard images affixed to the wall of the surgical room were captured from various angles [15]. Afterwards, the intrinsic camera parameters were calculated using OpenCV: $f_x = 489$, $f_y = 529$, $c_x = 369$, and $c_y = 277$. Three laparoscopic biopsy forceps with diameters of 4.6 mm, 4.7 mm, and 4.8 mm were used. Thirty videos, recorded between June 2020 and March 2023, were selected from two university hospitals and subsequently annotated. The training, validation, and test sets for Mask2Former were composed of 18, 6, and 6 videos containing 1304, 433, and 572 frames, respectively. The entire dataset comprised 27 distinct classes of organs and anatomical structures of the abdominal cavity, including, but not limited to, the liver, stomach, gallbladder, diaphragm, spleen, and bowels. The obtained Overall Accuracy, Mean IoU, Mean Accuracy, Mean Precision, and Mean Recall values across all classes were 77.61, 52.27, 63.94, 70.40, and 63.94, respectively. MiDaS, without any fine-tuning, was solely utilized as an inferencer to provide relative distances. Two highly experienced GI surgeons analyzed 18 laparoscopic videos, each featuring 1–4 biopsy procedures for PM. 76 frames containing a SI and a tumor were randomly chosen. We provide several images, along with corresponding depth information, segmentation outcomes, and the visual output of the newly developed measurement module, in Fig. 3. Figure 4 displays the estimates produced by the surgeons and our method, with tumor sizes ranging from 1.5 mm to 37.5 mm. Surgeons measured the length of a tumor either along the diagonal, horizontal, or vertical dimension of the bounding box, whereas the proposed method provided measurements for all three dimensions, enabling a comprehensive comparison. The obtained results demonstrate that our method is reliable, yielding an MAE [10] of 2.44 mm ± 0.23 mm.

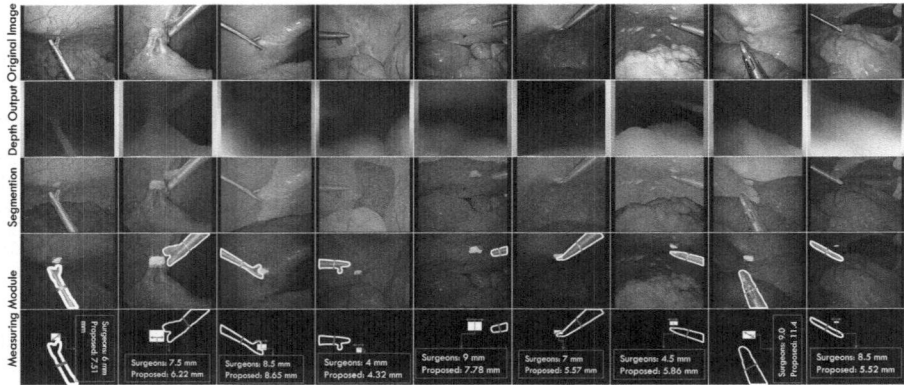

Fig. 3. Visual results: upon acquiring the output of MiDaS and Mask2Former, the measurement module determines the horizontal, vertical, and diagonal tumor length.

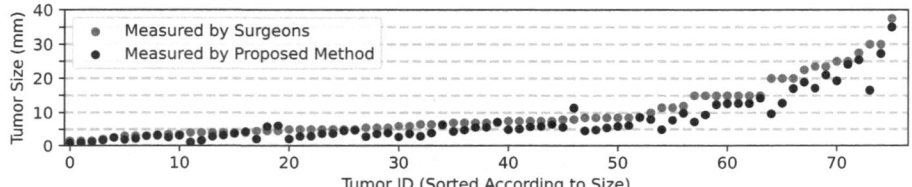

Fig. 4. Differences in tumor size estimates made by surgeons and our method.

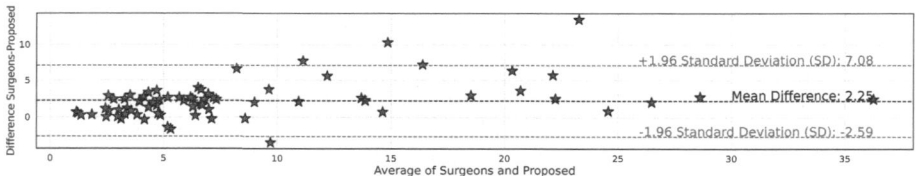

Fig. 5. Agreement between the tumor size estimates made by surgeons and our method.

We also show a Bland-Altman plot [1] in Fig. 5 to assess the agreement between the two employed measurement methods. Over 95% of the data points are within the agreement limits (mean difference ±1.96 times the standard deviation of the differences). 76.32% of the points are in the mean difference ±2 range, and there are just four outliers (out of mean difference ±1.96SD) among the 76 images. This means that the two ways of measuring are strongly in agreement.

5 Conclusions and Future Research

In this paper, we introduced a novel method for automatic size measurement of abdominal tumors in monocular laparoscopic videos. We achieved this by defining a mathematical relationship between target and reference objects, object segmentation, and depth estimation. The obtained experimental results indicate that the newly proposed method for tumor size measurement is accurate, with a MAE of 2.44 mm ± 0.23 mm.

In future research, we aim at determining depth information in the abdominal cavity by adopting self-supervised monocular depth estimation, as state-of-the-art depth estimators are trained on natural images. A second topic for future research is training a deep attention-based convolutional model to measure tumor size at various distances and viewpoints without any reference object.

The assumption that a tumor lies on a plane fronto-parallel to the image plane is a limitation, as it simplifies the problem by treating the tumor as if it is always viewed from a perpendicular angle. In practice, tumors may be viewed from skewed angles due to the positioning of the camera and the anatomy of the abdominal cavity. This can distort the shape and size of the tumor at hand, leading to inaccurate size estimation. Therefore, a final topic for future research involves developing methods to account for these skewed perspectives.

References

1. Altman, D.G., Bland, J.M.: Measurement in medicine: the analysis of method comparison studies. J. Royal Stat. Soc. Ser. D Stat. **32**(3), 307–317 (1983)
2. Alyami, M., et al.: Pressurised intraperitoneal aerosol chemotherapy: rationale, evidence, and potential indications. Lancet Oncol. **20**(7), e368–e377 (2019)
3. Andaló, F.A., Taubin, G., Goldenstein, S.: Efficient height measurements in single images based on the detection of vanishing points. Comput. Vis. Image Underst. **138**, 51–60 (2015)
4. Birkl, R., Wofk, D., Müller, M.: MiDaS v3. 1–a model zoo for robust monocular relative depth estimation. arXiv preprint arXiv:2307.14460 (2023)
5. Cheng, B., Misra, I., Schwing, A.G., Kirillov, A., Girdhar, R.: Masked-attention mask transformer for universal image segmentation. In: Proceedings of the IEEE/CVF Conference on Computer Vision and Pattern Recognition (CVPR), pp. 1290–1299, June 2022
6. Criminisi, A., Reid, I., Zisserman, A.: Single view metrology. Int. J. Comput. Vision **40**, 123–148 (2000)
7. Goldstein, O., Segol, O., Gross, S.A., Jacob, H., Siersema, P.D.: Novel device for measuring polyp size: an ex vivo animal study. Gut **67**, 1755–1756 (2018)
8. Harmon, R.L., Sugarbaker, P.H.: Prognostic indicators in peritoneal carcinomatosis from gastrointestinal cancer. In: International Seminars in Surgical Oncology, vol. 2, pp. 1–10. BioMed Central (2005)
9. Hartley, R., Zisserman, A.: Multiple View Geometry in Computer Vision, 2nd edn. Cambridge University Press, Cambridge (2003)
10. Iakovidis, D.K., Dimas, G., Karargyris, A., Bianchi, F., Ciuti, G., Koulaouzidis, A.: Deep endoscopic visual measurements. IEEE J. Biomed. Health Inform. **23**(6), 2211–2219 (2018)
11. Jacquet, P., Sugarbaker, P.H.: Clinical research methodologies in diagnosis and staging of patients with peritoneal carcinomatosis. In: Peritoneal Carcinomatosis: Principles of Management, pp. 359–374 (1996)

12. Oka, K., Seki, T., Akatsu, T., Wakabayashi, T., Inui, K., Yoshino, J.: Clinical study using novel endoscopic system for measuring size of gastrointestinal lesion. World J. Gastroenterol. WJG **20**(14), 4050 (2014)
13. Sugarbaker, P.H., Jablonski, K.A.: Prognostic features of 51 colorectal and 130 appendiceal cancer patients with peritoneal carcinomatosis treated by cytoreductive surgery and intraperitoneal chemotherapy. Ann. Surg. **221**(2), 124 (1995)
14. Visentini-Scarzanella, M., et al.: A structured light laser probe for gastrointestinal polyp size measurement: a preliminary comparative study. Endosc. Int. Open **6**(05), E602–E609 (2018)
15. Zhang, Z.: A flexible new technique for camera calibration. IEEE Trans. Pattern Anal. Mach. Intell. **22**(11), 1330–1334 (2000)
16. Zhang, Z., Han, Y., Zhou, Y., Dai, M.: A novel absolute localization estimation of a target with monocular vision. Optik **124**(12), 1218–1223 (2013)
17. Zhou, M., Bao, G., Geng, Y., Alkandari, B., Li, X.: Polyp detection and radius measurement in small intestine using video capsule endoscopy. In: 2014 7th International Conference on Biomedical Engineering and Informatics, pp. 237–241. IEEE (2014)

Follicular Lymphoma Grading Based on 3D-DDcGAN and Bayesian CNN Using PET-CT Images

Lulu He[1], Chunjun Qian[1], Yue Teng[2], Chongyang Ding[3], and Chong Jiang[4(✉)]

[1] Department of Automation, Hertfordshire College, Changzhou Institute of Technology, Changzhou 213032, Jiangsu, China
[2] Department of Nuclear Medicine, Nanjing Drum Tower Hospital, Nanjing 210008, Jiangsu, China
[3] Department of Nuclear Medicine, Jiangsu Province Hospital, Nanjing 210029, Jiangsu, China
[4] Department of Nuclear Medicine, West China Hospital, Chengdu 610041, Sichuan, China
jiangc_nju@163.com

Abstract. Follicular lymphoma (FL) is a non-Hodgkin lymphoma and an indolent B-cell lymphoproliferative disorder of transformed follicular center B cells. In the diagnosis, FL should be graded by counting the number of centroblasts in the pathological image, which is time-consuming. In this study, we try to propose a FL grading method based on the PET and CT images. We propose a 3D-DDcGAN to fuse the simultaneously collected PET and CT images. Then, the BayesianResNet18 (ResNet18 is improved by introducing Bayes' theorem) is adopted for the FL grading. Our method is trained and tested on mixed data consisting of FL grades I-III and DLBCL. Finally, the evaluation metrics for our method are accuracy 0.814, precision 0.782, recall 0.699, macro-averaged F1-score 0.731, and micro-averaged F1-score 0.817. The method based on deep learning and medical imaging will help assist in disease grading and developing personalized treatment plans.

Keywords: Follicular Lymphoma Grading · 3D-DDcGAN · Bayesian CNN

1 Introduction

Follicular lymphoma (FL) is the most common type of low-grade non-Hodgkin lymphoma (NHL) [1]. Generally, it is an indolent B-cell lymphoproliferative disorder of transformed follicular center B cells [2]. Much literature has reported that FL is the second most common lymphoma diagnosed in the United States and Western Europe [2,3]. This disease has been paid more and more attention in China. In [3], the authors collected the data of 1845 Chinese FL patients to study the clinical presentations, treatments, and prognosis. However, in the

© The Author(s), under exclusive license to Springer Nature Switzerland AG 2025
J. Wu et al. (Eds.): CMMCA 2024, LNCS 15181, pp. 21–30, 2025.
https://doi.org/10.1007/978-3-031-73360-4_3

diagnosis, FL should be graded through pathology [4], which is time-consuming because the common grading method is based on the number of centroblasts in the pathological image [2]. According to the grading system used by the WHO Classification, FL can be divided into grades I–III. However, grade III will be further subdivided into grades IIIa and IIIb. Grade IIIb FL is more like diffuse large B cell lymphoma (DLBCL) and is treated as such [5]. Therefore, accurately identifying the subtype of FL is useful in deciding on a treatment plan.

With the development of machine learning or deep learning methods, many different neural networks have been proposed or applied in medical image analysis. To discriminate FL from DLBCL, de Jesus et al. [6] proposed the machine learning-based model to analyze the extracted radiomic features. In [7], researchers considered using multimodal deep learning to predict the primary treatment failure in DLBCL. However, in this study, we consider the FL subtype classification through image fusion and classification. In the field of medical image fusion, many methods have been proposed, especially generative adversarial networks (GAN). A GAN-based image fusion model often comprises a generator and a discriminator. There are many architectures for generators and discriminators, such as Wasserstein GAN (WGAN) [8], conditional GAN (cGAN), and U-Patch GAN [9]. The most used GAN model in the medical image fusion field is cGAN. Based on the cGAN, many different improved fusion models have been proposed, such as dual-discriminator cGAN (DDcGAN) [10, 11], multi-generator multi-discriminator cGAN (MGMDcGAN) [12], deep cGAN (DCGAN) [13]. Except for these algorithm improvements, other GAN-based medical image fusion models were developed for special applications, i.e., cell image fusion [14], medical image synthesis [15], medical image fusion quality assessment [16], medical image translation [17], and brain tumors in multi-modal MRI [18, 19]. However, these image fusion-based applications do not refer to disease grading.

Disease grading is challenging in clinical diagnosis or medical image analysis. An accurate grading system helps develop a personalized treatment plan. In recent years, scholars have made much more effort in accurate grading system development based on medical images for some cancer diseases, such as prostate cancer [20] and breast cancer [21, 22]. Among these grading systems, CNN is the commonly considered baseline model. Inspired by these methods, we improved the DDcGAN [10] to achieve the image fusion for PET and CT and introduced a Bayesian CNN (BCNN) [23] based on the fused images for the FL grading.

2   Method

This section introduces our FL grading method, including an improved DDcGAN to fuse the PET and CT images and a BCNN responsible for FL grading. Figure 1 shows the overview of our method, the architecture of 3D-DDcGAN, and the diagram of BCNN.

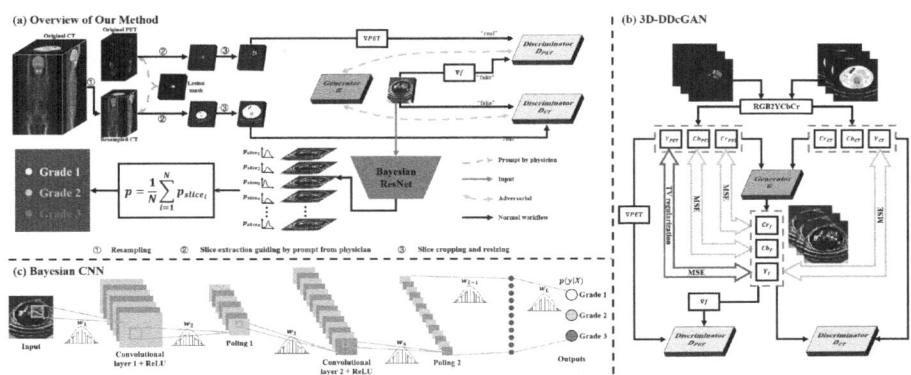

Fig. 1. Overview of our method. (b) The architecture of 3D-DDcGAN. Right-angled bidirectional arrows indicate direct loss calculations between each other. RGB2YCbCr operation transforms the image from RGB channels into YCbCr space. MSE means the mean square error. ∇PET and ∇f are the gradients of the PET and generated images. (c) The diagram of BCNN. The input is the fused image from 3D-DDcGAN, and the outputs are the probabilities that the input belongs to the three categories. w_i is the weight parameters in the i-th layer. In the BCNN, weight parameters are computed by the posterior predictive distribution on drawing samples. L means the number of layers.

2.1 3D-DDcGAN

Given a pair of aligned PET image PET and CT image CT, the whole procedure of our 3D-DDcGAN is shown in Fig. 1(b). Our 3D-DDcGAN aims to learn a generator network G conditioned on the PET and CT with three channels. Through the G, we can obtain the fused image $f = G(PET, CT)$. We adopt two discriminators D_{PET} and D_{CT} to obtain a more informative fusion image, as in the DDcGAN [10]. D_{PET} is trained to discriminate between the gradient of the generated image ∇f and the gradient of the PET image ∇PET, which can merge grayscale change information of the PET image into the generated image f. Considering that less grayscale variation in CT, as shown in Step ③ of Fig. 1(a), we do not calculate the gradient of CT. The role of D_{CT} is to distinguish the generated image f from CT, which can introduce the structure information of CT into the generated image f.

In our 3D-DDcGAN, the adversarial relationship can be formulated as

$$\min_{G} \max_{D_{PET}, D_{CT}} E[\log D_{PET}(\nabla PET)] + E[\log(1 - D_{PET}(\nabla f))] \\ + E[\log D_{CT}(CT)] + E[\log(1 - D_{CT}(f))]. \tag{1}$$

The probability distributions of the gradients of the PET image ∇PET and generated image ∇f are denoted as $P(\nabla PET)$ and $P(\nabla f)$, respectively. The probability distributions of CT and generated image f are denoted as $P(CT)$ and $P(f)$, respectively. The divergence between $P(\nabla f)$ and $P(\nabla PET)$ and the divergence between $P(f)$ and $P(CT)$ will decrease simultaneously through the adversarial process.

The loss function in our 3D-DDcGAN training is defined as follows:

$$\mathcal{L} = \mathcal{L}_G^{adv} + \lambda\mathcal{L}_{reg} + \alpha\mathcal{L}_{MSE} + \beta\mathcal{L}_{chro}, \qquad (2)$$
$$\alpha + \beta = 1,$$

where λ, α and β are hyper-parameters to control the trade-off. $\mathcal{L}_G^{adv}$ comes from discriminators and is defined as $\mathcal{L}_G^{adv} = E[\log(1 - D_{PET}(\nabla f))] + E[\log(1 - D_{CT}(f))]$. The second term in Eq. (2) is a TV regularization to preserve the similar grayscale variation in the fused image as in the PET image, which is defined as $\mathcal{L}_{reg} = E[|||f - Y_{PET}||_{TV}]$.

The third term in Eq. (2) is a similarity constraint formulated by mean square error (MSE) $\mathcal{L}_{MSE} = \omega_{Y_{PET}}\mathcal{L}_{sim}(f, Y_{PET}) + \omega_{Y_{CT}}\mathcal{L}_{sim}(f, Y_{CT})$ [24] is adopted. $\mathcal{L}_{sim}(f, \cdot)$ is mathematically defined as $\mathcal{L}_{sim}(f, \cdot) = \frac{\epsilon}{HW}||f - \cdot||_F^2$. ϵ is a hyper-parameter, and $|| \cdot ||_F$ means the Frobenius norm. Y_{CT} is the Y channel of the CT image. H and W are the height and width of the images. $\omega_{Y_{PET}}$ and $\omega_{Y_{CT}}$ are, respectively, the importance weights defined by the surface-level measurement results of Y_{PET} and Y_{CT}. The surface-level measurement consists of saliency and abundance measurements, which can be calculated by Sign function and entropy as $m_{Image}^{saliency} = \frac{1}{HW}\sum_{i=1}^{H}\sum_{j=1}^{W}\frac{\text{Sign}(Image_{i,j}-\tau)+1}{2} \cdot Image_{i,j}$ and $m_{Image}^{abundance} = -\sum_{l=0}^{L}p_l^{Image}\log_2 p_l^{Image}$, where τ means the threshold to screen for salient regions, and $\text{Sign}(\cdot)$ is Sign function. (i, j) is the coordinate of the pixel in the $Image$ such as Y_{PET} or Y_{CT}. L is the number of gray levels and set as 256, and p_l is the probability of the l-th gray level in $Image$. Then, we can calculate $\omega_{Y_{PET}}$ and $\omega_{Y_{CT}}$ by the formula $\omega_{Image} = \frac{e^{\frac{s_{Image}}{\eta}}}{e^{\frac{s_{PET}}{\eta}}+e^{\frac{s_{CT}}{\eta}}}$, which can ensure that $\omega_{Y_{PET}} + \omega_{Y_{CT}} = 1$ and $0 < \omega_{Y_{PET}}, \omega_{Y_{CT}} < 1$. η is defined as a control parameter to measure the scaling of the difference between $s_{Y_{PET}}$ and $s_{Y_{CT}}$, which are calculated by $s_{Y_{PET}} = \psi m_{Y_{PET}}^{saliency} + m_{Y_{PET}}^{abundance}$ and $s_{Y_{CT}} = \psi m_{Y_{CT}}^{saliency} + m_{Y_{CT}}^{abundance}$, ψ is a hyper-parameter to control the trade-off between two measurement ways.

In our loss function, the chrominance constraint is adopted and defined as $\mathcal{L}_{chro} = \frac{1}{HW}||Cb_f - Cb_{PET}||_F^2 + \frac{1}{HW}||Cr_f - Cr_{PET}||_F^2$, where Cb_f and Cr_f are the Cb and Cr channels of generated image f by generator G. Cb_{PET} and Cr_{PET} are that of PET image. It is to be noted that we only retain the chrominance information of the PET image, which can provide more intuitive information for FL grading.

2.2   BCNN-Based Grading

Depending on severity, FL is divided into grades I, II, and III. In our study, Grade I consists of FL1 and FL2 [25]. Grade II refers to FL3a, and Grade III is FL3b [25]. Grades I and II are often indistinguishable because of the close relationship in the histological FL subtypes [25]. From a cognitive perspective, there is uncertainty between Grades I and II, and this uncertainty can lead the model to bias the recognition results of different grades of FL towards DLBCL. Here, we consider uncertainty estimation [23] based on Bayes' theorem but do not simply implement CNN to divide FL into three categories.

BCNN [23] (Fig. 1(c)) tries to compute the posterior probabilities of the weight parameters based on the posterior predictive distribution, which can prevent overfitting in the small dataset. Suppose that $D = \{X_i, y_i\}$, and X_i is the fused FL image with label y_i. Further, suppose that w is the weight parameter of a CNN. According to Bayes' theorem, we can obtain that $p(w|D) \propto p(D|w)p(w)$, where $p(D|w) = \Pi_i p(y_i|X_i, w)$. The maximum a posteriori estimate of w can be obtained by maximizing $p(D|w)p(w)$. Then, we can make predictions by considering the weight uncertainty with a full posterior distribution of w.

The posterior $p(w|D)$ is untractable, and a variational distribution $q(w|\theta)$ is often used to approximate the true posterior $p(w|D)$. Here, the Kullback-Leibler divergence is used as a loss function between $q(w|\theta)$ and $p(w|D)$, together with Bayes' theorem to $p(w|D)$, which can be formulated as:

$$\text{KL}[q(w|\theta)||p(w|D)] = \text{KL}[q(w|\theta)||p(w)] - E_{q(w|\theta)}[\log p(D|w)] + \log p(D). \quad (3)$$

The first two terms are the variational free energy $F(D, \theta)$, and $\log p(D)$ is known and independent on w. Equation (3) can be rewritten into the following form:

$$\text{KL}[q(w|\theta)||p(w|D)] = F(D, \theta) + \log p(D). \quad (4)$$

Therefore, minimizing the $\text{KL}[q(w|\theta)||p(w|D)]$ can be transformed as minimizing the $F(D, \theta) = \text{KL}[q(w|\theta)||p(w)] - E_{q(w|\theta)}[\log p(D|w)]$. By rearranging the KL term in $F(D, \theta)$, we can obtain

$$F(D, \theta) = E_{q(w|\theta)} \log q(w|\theta) - E_{q(w|\theta)} \log p(w) - E_{q(w|\theta)}[\log p(D|w)]. \quad (5)$$

For the training dataset $D = \{X_i, y_i\}$, Eq. (5) can be approximated by drawing samples w_i from $q(w|\theta)$ as $F(D, \theta) \approx \frac{1}{N} \sum_{i=1}^{N} [\log q(w_i|\theta) - \log p(w_i) - \log p(D|w_i)]$. The first term can be calculated as $\log q(w_i|\theta) = \log \mathcal{N}(w_i|\mu, \sigma_q^2)$, which is a variational posterior with mean μ and standard σ_q. The second term is the log prior $\log p(w_i) = \log \mathcal{N}(w_i|0, \sigma_p^2)$, which is a zero-mean Gaussian distribution with standard σ_p. The third term is the likelihood $\log p(D|w_i)$, which is the network output.

3   Experiments

3.1   Data Sets and Evaluation Metrics

All the data in this study were collected from three medical imaging centers: West China Hospital, Nanjing Drum Tower Hospital, and Jiangsu Province Hospital. All patients fasted for at least 6 h before scans, resulting in blood glucose levels under 8.7 mmol/L. Then, 185–370 MBq of [18F]FDG (5.18 MBq/kg) was administered intravenously. The PET/CT scans (from the base of the skull to the upper thigh) were performed 60 min after the radiopharmaceutical injection. Emission data were acquired for 2 min in each bed position. All patients underwent PET/CT scans with one of the following systems: UM780 PET/CT and GE discovery PET/CT clarity 710, Biograph 16 PET/CT, and Gemini GXL. CT acquisition data were used for attenuation correction. All PET/CT images are jointly reviewed by two attending nuclear medicine specialists with 8 years of experience. In cases of disagreement, a senior nuclear medicine physician participated and made the final decision. The lesion regions in our collected datasets were manually delineated using LIFEx-7.3.0 software (https://www.lifexsoft.org/) on the PET images. All PET and CT images were collected almost simultaneously but did not match perfectly. Considering all the lesion regions were outlined on PET images, we regarded PET as the reference image and CT as the moving one. Then, we used a simple 3D rigid registration method "elastix" (a Python library)[1], to achieve the image registration from CT to PET. We collected 837 3D PET and CT images, and Table 1 shows the detailed category distribution from three imaging centers. To ensure the data balance and effectively identify the Grade III (FL3b, more like DLBCL [2]), we randomly selected 458 DLBCL patients' data from our previous work [26]. We adopt the accuracy, precision, recall, macro-averaged F1-score (macro-F1) and micro-averaged F1-score (micro-F1) for the evaluation metrics.

Table 1. Detailed category distribution from three imaging centers.

Center	Category			
	Grade I	Grade II	Grade III	DLBCL
West China Hospital	89	62	40	200
Nanjing Drum Tower Hospital	56	13	2	108
Jiangsu Province Hospital	76	26	15	150

3.2 Experimental Settings

Our method consists of two different neural networks, including 3D-DDcGAN and BCNN. The model training and testing of both neural networks and other compared methods are taken on an NVIDIA RTX3090 GPU. In the implementation, we extract all the lesion slices from the resampled 3D images according to the lesion ROI by the physicians. Then, we mix the data from three different centers by category and divide each category into training and testing sets in a 3:7 ratio. In the training stage, 25% of the training set is randomly selected as the validation set. It is to be noted that the input in the training and testing

---

[1] https://simpleelastix.github.io/.

stage is a 2D image, but the testing result is a mean probability from all the probabilities of 2D lesion ROIs in a given 3D image.

For both neural network training, the batch size is 32. The hyper-parameters in Eq. (2) are set as $\lambda = 1.2$, $\alpha = 0.2$, and $\beta = 0.8$. To be noted that the setting of λ is from [10] without any modification, and α and β are obtained from the experiments to control the value of α. The ϵ in $\mathcal{L}_{sim}(f, \cdot)$ of the third term in Eq. (2) and η in the calculation of ω_{Image} are set as 1. ψ in $S_{Y_{PET}}$ and $S_{Y_{CT}}$ calculations is set as 3, which is the same as that in [24]. The optimizers are "RMSProp" in the generator and "GradientDescent" in two discriminators with an initial learning rate of 0.0002. During the training process, the learning rate is set to decay exponentially with a decay rate of 0.9 as the number of batches changes. For the BCNN training, we use the optimizer "SGD" with an initial learning rate of 0.002 in a bone architecture of ResNet18 (BayesianResNet18). The loss function for the output in the BCNN is categorical cross-entropy. Finally, we obtain a 4-class classifier to identify Grades I-III of FL and DLBCL.

In the comparison experiments, we consider the different fusion strategies, such as AddingFusion, EMFusion [24], and our 3D-DDcGAN. AddingFusion implements the intensities of adding operation at the same coordinate position in CT and PET images. For the EMFusion [24], we directly use the trained model[2], but the inputs are PET image with RGB three channels and CT gray-level image. We also conduct experiments on single-modality images to demonstrate the contribution of fused images in grading.

3.3   Results and Discussion

In Fig. 2, some visual examples are displayed. PET, CT, and fused images with different fusion methods belong to four different grades, which can be seen in Fig. 2. The red regions in PET images are lesions, and CT images provide almost no information that helps identify lesions. For AddingFusion and EMFusion [24], the lesion regions can be highlighted in the generated fused images, but no more discriminative visual features can be provided.

Table 2 shows the evaluation metrics from different methods. Our methods, 3D-DDcGAN+ResNet18 and 3D-DDcGAN+BayesianResNet18, are superior to other methods. From the evaluation metrics, ResNet18 can be improved by introducing Bayes' theorem and obtaining a better performance, compared with that without Bayes' theorem.

The results in Table 2 also indicate that PET images can provide more useful information in FL grading, and different fusion strategies can reach different grading results. If an inappropriate fusion method (i.e., AddingFusion) is used or a fusion method (i.e., EMFusion [24]) is not re-trained for specific applications, the effectiveness of the grading method will decrease. In contrast, if a useful fusion method is adopted, the grading results are better than those from the single-modality images. In addition, Bayes' theorem may not improve the performance of ResNet18 on some images, such as PET images and fused images

---

[2] https://github.com/hanna-xu/EMFusion.

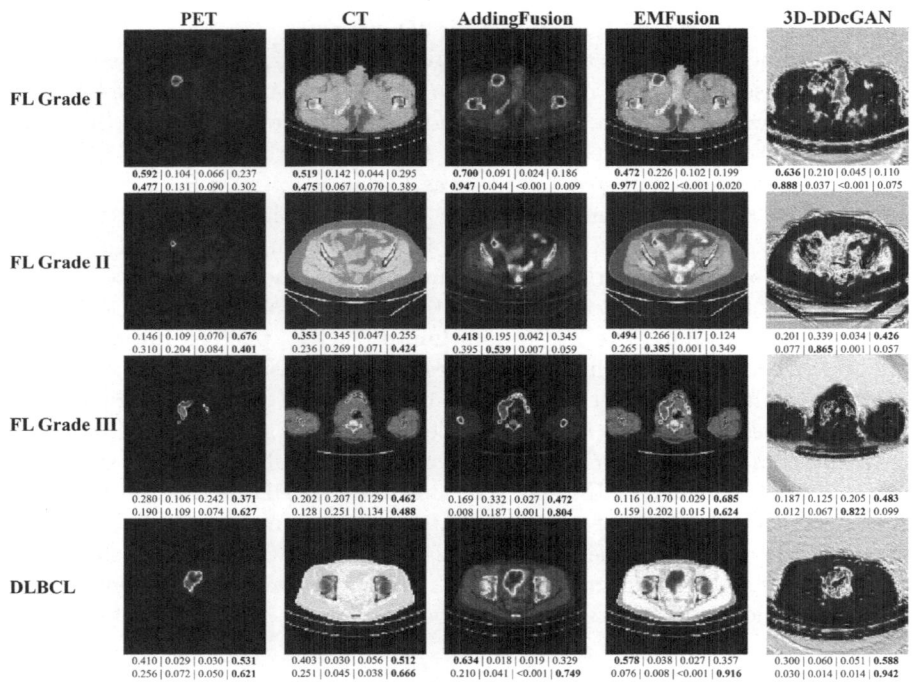

Fig. 2. Some visual examples in pseudo color. Under each image, the prediction results by ResNet18 (first row) and BayesianResNet18 (second row) in four categories are provided, and bold font indicates the final predicted grading results.

Table 2. Evaluation metrics on our dataset.

Method	Evaluation Metric				
	Accuracy	Precision	Recall	macro-F1	micro-F1
CT+ResNet18	0.509	0.267	0.263	0.231	0.511
CT+BayesianResNet18	0.573	0.348	0.296	0.263	0.560
PET+ResNet18	0.673	0.450	0.435	0.417	0.638
PET+BayesianResNet18	0.611	0.293	0.359	0.322	0.583
AddingFusion+ResNet18	0.544	0.332	0.327	0.320	0.556
AddingFusion+BayesianResNet18	0.536	0.375	0.350	0.354	0.539
EMFusion [24]+ResNet18	0.498	0.305	0.285	0.276	0.499
EMFusion [24]+BayesianResNet18	0.546	0.371	0.333	0.331	0.524
3D-DDcGAN+ResNet18	0.709	0.770	0.491	0.511	0.707
3D-DDcGAN+BayesianResNet18	**0.814**	**0.782**	**0.699**	**0.731**	**0.817**

obtained by the AddingFusion strategy. The deep learning method will help assist in disease grading, which will be useful in developing personalized treatment plans. If the accuracy of the model reaches the level of pathological results, early prediction of FL subtypes can be made and personalized treatment plans can be guided. To achieve improved results in FL grading, we will further focus on image fusion and classification methods in the future.

4   Conclusion

This study proposes an FL grading method, including the image fusion between PET and CT, and FL grading by a classification method. We propose a 3D-DDcGAN to generate the fused images and introduce Bayes' theorem into ResNet18 architecture (BayesianResNet18) for FL grading. Some comparison experiment results demonstrate that our method performs better in FL grading.

Acknowledgments. This study was funded by the National Natural Science of China (Grant NO. 62201095) and Changzhou Leading Innovative Talents Introduction and Cultivation Project (Grant No. CQ20210097).

References

1. Li, Y., Zhang, Y., Wang, W., et al.: Follicular lymphoma in China: systematic evaluation of follicular lymphoma prognostic models. Cancer Manage. Res. **14**, 1385–1393 (2023)
2. Freedman, A., Jacobsen, E.: Follicular lymphoma: update on diagnosis and management. Am. J. Hematol. **95**(2020), 316–327 (2020)
3. Zha, J., Fan, L., Yi, S., et al.: Clinical features and outcomes of 1845 patients with follicular lymphoma: a real-world multicenter experience in China. J. Hematol. Oncol. **14**, 131 (2021)
4. Randall, C., Fedoriw, Y.: Pathology and diagnosis of follicular lymphoma and related entities. Pathology **52**(1), 30–39 (2020)
5. Swerdlow, S.H., Campo, E., Pileri, S.A., et al.: The 2016 revision of the World Health Organization classification of lymphoid neoplasms. Blood **127**(20), 2375–2390 (2016)
6. de Jesus, F.M., Yin, Y., Mantzorou-Kyriaki, E., et al.: Machine learning in the differentiation of follicular lymphoma from diffuse large B-cell lymphoma with radiomic [18F]FDG PET/CT features. Eur. J. Nucl. Med. Mol. Imaging **49**, 1535–1543 (2022)
7. Yuan, C., Shi, Q., Huang, X., et al.: Multimodal deep learning model on interim [18F]FDG PET/CT for predicting primary treatment failure in diffuse large B-cell lymphoma. Eur. Radiol. **33**, 77–88 (2023)
8. Yang, Z., Chen, Y., Le, Z., et al.: Multi-source medical image fusion based on Wasserstein generative adversarial networks. IEEE Access **7**, 175947–175958 (2019)
9. Fan, C., Lin, H., Qiu, Y.: U-patch GAN: a medical image fusion method based on GAN. J. Digit. Imaging **36**, 339–355 (2023)
10. Xu, H., Liang, P., Yu, W., et al.: Learning a generative model for fusing infrared and visible images via conditional generative adversarial network with dual discriminators. In: IJCAI, pp. 3954–3960 (2019)

11. Ma, J., Xu, H., Jiang, J., et al.: DDcGAN: a dual-discriminator conditional generative adversarial network for multi-resolution image fusion. IEEE Trans. Image Process. **29**, 4980–4995 (2020)
12. Huang, J., Le, Z., Ma, Y., et al.: MGMDcGAN: medical image fusion using multi-generator multi-discriminator conditional generative adversarial network. IEEE Access **8**, 55145–55157 (2020)
13. Zhao, C., Wang, T., Lei, B.: Medical image fusion method based on dense block and deep convolutional generative adversarial network. Neural Comput. Appl. **33**, 6595–6610 (2021)
14. Tang, W., Liu, Y., Zhang, C., et al.: Green fluorescent protein and phase-contrast image fusion via generative adversarial networks. Comput. Math. Methods Med. **2019**, 5450373 (2019)
15. Wang, C., Yang, G., Papanastasiou, G., et al.: DiCyc: GAN-based deformation invariant cross-domain information fusion for medical image synthesis. Inf. Fusion **67**, 147–160 (2021)
16. Tang, L., Hui, Y., Yang, H., et al.: Medical image fusion quality assessment based on conditional generative adversarial network. Front. Neurosci. **9**(16), 986153 (2022)
17. Amirkolaee, H.A., Amirkolaee, H.A.: Medical image translation using an edge-guided generative adversarial network with global-to-local feature fusion. J. Biomed. Res. **36**(6), 409–422 (2022)
18. Huang, P., Li, D., Jiao, Z., et al.: Common feature learning for brain tumor MRI synthesis by context-aware generative adversarial network. Med. Image Anal. **79**, 102472 (2022)
19. Liu, X., Chen, H., Yao, C., et al.: BTMF-GAN: a multi-modal MRI fusion generative adversarial network for brain tumors. Comput. Biol. Med. **157**, 106769 (2023)
20. Vente, C.d., Vos, P., Hosseinzadeh, M., et al.: Deep learning regression for prostate cancer detection and grading in Bi-parametric MRI. IEEE Trans. Biomed. Eng. **68**(2), 374–383 (2021)
21. Fan, M., Yuan, C., Huang, G., et al.: A framework for deep multitask learning with multiparametric magnetic resonance imaging for the joint prediction of histological characteristics in breast cancer. IEEE J. Biomed. Health Inform. **26**(8), 3884–3895 (2022)
22. Sun, R., Wei, L., Hou, X., et al.: Molecular-subtype guided automatic invasive breast cancer grading using dynamic contrast-enhanced MRI. Comput. Methods Programs Biomed. **242**, 107804 (2023)
23. Shridhar, K., Laumann, F., Liwicki, M.: A comprehensive guide to Bayesian convolutional neural network with variational inference. arXiv preprint arXiv:1901.02731 (2019)
24. Xu, H., Ma, J.: EMFusion: an unsupervised enhanced medical image fusion network. Inf. Fusion **76**, 177–186 (2021)
25. Horn, H., Kohler, C., Witzig, R., et al.: Gene expression profiling reveals a close relationship between follicular lymphoma grade 3A and 3B, but distinct profiles of follicular lymphoma grade 1 and 2. Haematologica **103**(7), 1182–1190 (2018)
26. Jiang, C., Qian, C., Jiang, Z., et al.: Robust deep learning-based PET prognostic imaging biomarker for DLBCL patients: a multicenter study. Eur. J. Nucl. Med. Mol. Imaging **50**, 3949–3960 (2023)

Multi-channel Multi-model Fusion Module (MMFM) Based Circulating Abnormal Cells (CACs) Detection for Lung Cancer Early Diagnosis with Fluorescence in Situ Hybridization (FISH) Images

Yinglan Kuang[1], Huajia Wang[1], Yanling Zhou[1], Xin Ye[2], and Xing Lu[1,2(✉)]

[1] ZhuhaiHengqin Sanmed Aitech Ltd., Zhuhai, Guangdong, China
lv.xing@sanmedbio.com
[2] ZhuhaiSanmed Biotech Inc., Zhuhai, Guangdong, China

Abstract. The accurate identification of circulating abnormal cells (CACs) in four-color fluorescence images is highly dependent on the fluorescence expression under each channel. Previous studies have utilized instance segmentation and target detection algorithms to identify cells and signal points in four-color fluorescence in situ hybridization (FISH) microscopy images. However, these algorithms require high accuracy in cell edge segmentation and signal point detection, which hinders the success of CAC detection. In this study, we propose a novel method for discriminating CAC cells using four-color fluorescence channels and the fusion of information from different models based on previous techniques. In particular, we utilize the information distribution of the four-color fluorescence channels to train the MMFM-DL network and MMFM-ML model, respectively. Thereafter, the model fusion strategy is employed to enhance the performance of the deep learning and shallow machine learning methods, thereby achieving a more comprehensive and accurate identification of CACs. This method requires the interpretation of only 0.92% of the cells in the microscopy images of four-color fluorescence in situ hybridization, thereby ensuring that the CAC recall rate is guaranteed to be over 98%. This is a significant improvement over the previous method.

Keywords: Circulating Abnormal Cells · Abnormal Cell Detection · Model Fusion · Fluorescence In Situ Hybridization (FISH) Images Analysis

1 Introduction

Liquid biopsy techniques permit the detection of circulating abnormal cells (CACs) in blood, which have been proven to be important biomarkers for early lung cancer diagnosis [1–3]. The criterion for identifying circulating abnormal cells relies on fluorescence expression across multiple channels, necessitating accurate identification from tens of thousands of cells using four-color fluorescence in situ hybridization (FISH) [4, 5] to

© The Author(s), under exclusive license to Springer Nature Switzerland AG 2025
J. Wu et al. (Eds.): CMMCA 2024, LNCS 15181, pp. 31–40, 2025.
https://doi.org/10.1007/978-3-031-73360-4_4

achieve high-quality results. However, when fluorescence signals from FISH are used to identify CACs [6–10], various experimental factors, such as environmental conditions and raw material quality, may introduce background noise and impurities. This affects the accuracy of abnormal cell identification, leading to a high number of cells requiring manual review, thereby reducing efficiency and throughput.

Previously, Xu and Wang et al. proposed a method involving an instance segmentation algorithm to segment and localize cells, followed by a target detection algorithm to identify signal points in each fluorescence channel. They determined whether cells were CACs based on the number of signal points detected per channel [11–14]. However, the performance of this method is highly dependent on the accurate identification of signal points. Inaccurate identification can lead to misclassification and false positives, resulting in a high number of cells needing review.

To address this, we propose a CAC cell discrimination method based on the fusion of information from four fluorescence channels. This method significantly reduces the number of cells requiring manual review, thereby improving work efficiency. Information fusion is crucial in the design and optimization of artificial intelligence models. Li et al. [15] introduced an attentional mechanism that assigns different weights to feature maps with various receptive fields, which are then combined into a single feature map. Another common method for information fusion is increasing the number of features describing the image without increasing the information within each feature. Gao et al. [16] compared the concatenation module and the element-sum module, finding the concatenation module to be superior. Howard et al. [17] decomposed the complete convolution operation into Depthwise and Pointwise convolutions, allowing for multi-channel inputs to produce multi-channel outputs by convolving a channel with a single kernel and then combining them in the depth direction.

In our study, to fully leverage cell-level information from different fluorescence channels, we developed a deep learning-based network for CAC cell classification, integrating information from four fluorescence channels. Additionally, we trained a machine learning-based model for CAC cell classification based on cell-level features from different channels. Finally, a higher-level fusion of these two models was implemented to enhance overall performance. Various fusion strategies were evaluated in this study to provide insights into the mechanisms of information fusion, aiming to find the optimal approach.

2 Method

In this study, we propose a CAC classification method based on multi-channel multi-model fusion (MMFM) (see Fig. 1). Our approach integrates deep learning and machine learning methodologies that facilitate information fusion across distinct channels. The two models produce a complementary effect, which not only improves the CAC classification performance but also significantly enhances the efficiency of manual interpretation.

a) Framework

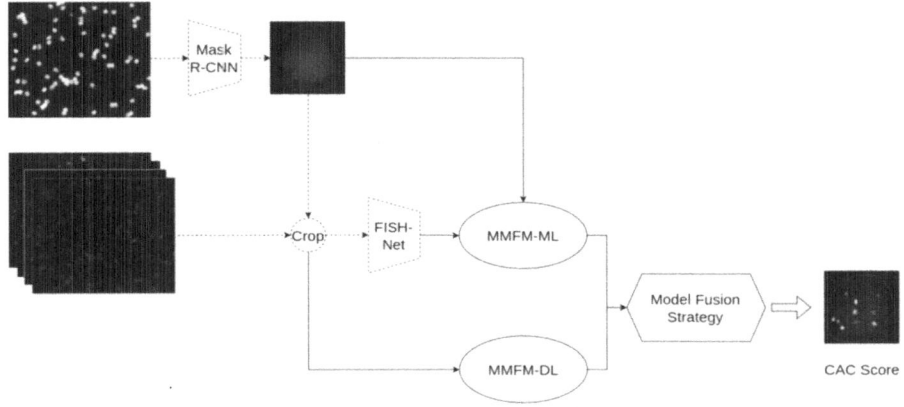

b) MMFM-DL

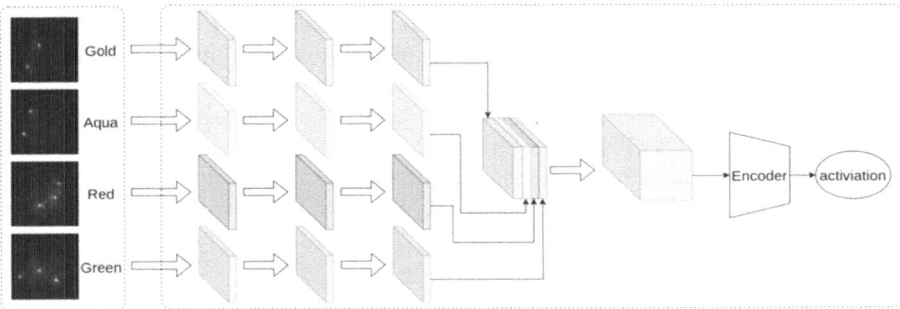

c) MMFM-ML

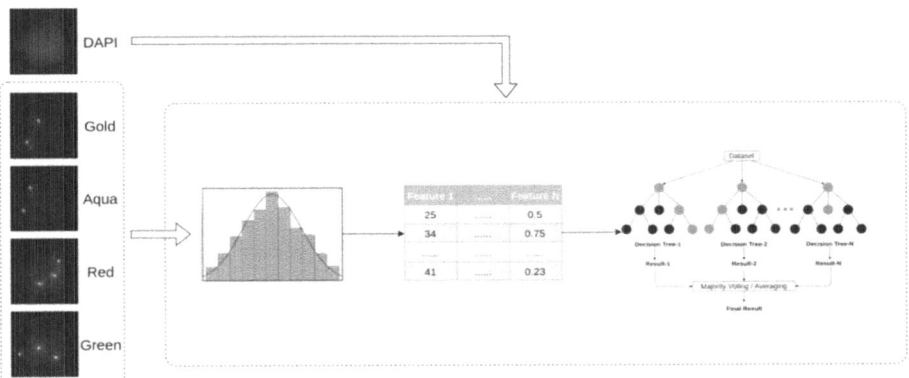

Fig. 1. The framework of the CAC classification method. a) After cell segmentation and signal point detection for each cell image, the multi-channel cell images are cropped to train MMFM-DL network, while multi-channel features are extracted to train MMFM-ML model, and the results of the two models are fused. b) Extract and combine features using the CACs Patch Partition module before accessing the classification network. c) Extract the morphological and textural features distribution of cells and and four-color fluorescent channel signal points through feature engineering and select the key features to train the random forest model.

2.1 Cell Segmentation and Signal Point Detection Network

The cell segmentation and signal point detection network employs the methodology proposed by Xu and Wang et al. [11–14] Building upon the enhanced MaskRCNN approach for delineating and localizing cells, the optimized YOLO algorithm (FISH-Net) utilized to identify the signal points in each fluorescence channel of the cell. Ultimately, the cell's categorization as a CAC cell was determined based on the number of signal points detected in each channel.

2.2 MMFM-DL Based CAC Classification Network

The fundamental concept of the MMFM-DL network is to extract the information of each channel independently through deep separable convolution, and then perform deep feature extraction to complete the classification. The architecture of MMFM-DL includes the CACs Patch Partition module, encoder, and fully connected layer. The mask from cell segmentation is employed to partition the four-color fluorescence channel map corresponding to each cell as input. The CACs Patch Partition module employs three layers of depth convolution [18] to extract features from the four-color fluorescence channel images independently, thereby ensuring that the features extracted from each channel are not interfering with each other. The depth features of the four-color fluorescence channels are then fused. The encoder is employed to extract the deep feature representations of the fused features. The Swin Transformer v2 [19, 20] has superior feature extraction capabilities in comparison to general convolutional neural networks, thus it is utilized in this context. Finally, two fully connected layers are utilized to accomplish the CAC classification task.

2.3 MMFM-ML Based CAC Classification Model

The morphological and textural features of cells and the four-color fluorescent channel signal points can be extracted from the cell segmentation network and signal point detection network, respectively. A total of 57 features are extracted for each cell, while 16 features are extracted for each fluorescent signal point. Each fluorescence channel of the cell will have zero or more signal points. The information distribution features of the four-color fluorescence channel were constructed by calculating the distribution of features (minimum, maximum, median, mean, and variance) under each fluorescence channel. Finally, 320 features were extracted, as detailed in Supplementary Table 1.

In this study, the Synthetic Small Number of Populations Transitional Sampling Technique (SMOTE) [21] was employed to effectively address the issue of sample imbalance, thereby increasing the sample size to 4096 cells for robust data analysis. The SMOTE algorithm in the Scikit-learn library employs a k-nearest neighbor algorithm to generate new data points based on the features of the underrepresented individuals. To extract key features, a random forest-based embedded feature selection method was employed to select 64 key features from 320 features. The selected key features were then input into the random forest model to train the MMFM-ML model.

2.4   Model Fusion Strategies

In this study, we examine three strategies for integrating the MMFM-DL and MMFM-ML models: average fusion, maximum fusion, and post-fusion. Prior to selecting a method, it is essential to evaluate the relative merits and drawbacks of each approach. In order to implement average fusion and maximum value fusion, it is necessary to train the MMFM-DL model and the MMFM-ML model, respectively. In mean fusion, the final cell classification probability is derived from the average of the predicted probabilities of the two models. In maximal fusion, the final cell classification probability is derived from the maximum of the predicted probabilities of the two models. In contrast, post-fusion necessitates the construction of the MMFM-DL model before training the MMFM-ML model using the predicted probability of deep learning as a key feature of the machine learning model.

3   Experiments and Results

3.1   Data Description

The dataset in this study was collected from 100 participants from different hospitals. Initially, 10 ml of peripheral blood were collected in ethylenediaminetetraacetic acid (EDTA) tubes initially. The samples were enriched by the Ficoll-Hypaque density gradient separation method and then the peripheral blood mononuclear cells (PBMCs) were deposited onto microscope glass slides using the Cytospin system (Thermo Fisher, Massachusetts, USA). Subsequently, the nuclei stained with DAPI, and the cells were hybridized with a 4-color FISH probe set (Sanmed Biotechnology Inc., Zhuhai, China), including the locus-specific identifier 3p22.1 (red), subtelomeric 3q29 (196F4, green), the locus-specific identifier 10q22.3 (gold) and centromere 10 (CEP10, aqua). Finally, the FISH samples were digitalized by Duet System (BioView Ltd., Allegro plus, ISR) to detect FISH signals. The number of FISH images per sample is mostly between 90 and 200, and the dimension of the image is 2448*2048.

The 100 participants were randomly divided into two groups. To address the issue of extreme sample imbalance, the FISH images containing CACs in each group were extracted to form a training set (315 frames) and a test set (303 frames). As previously stated, the training and validation sets are not complete FISH samples. In order to assess the efficacy of the proposed method in practical applications, an additional 10 participants were selected as the test set. All CACs were interpreted and confirmed by five to six experienced FISH image diagnostic experts.

3.2   Experimental Setting

During the training process of the MMFM-DL network, each fluorescence signal image was enhanced through the application of resizing, normalization, and grayscale conversion to enhance the robustness of the training process. The cross entropy loss function was employed, and label_smoothing was set to 0.1. The stochastic gradient descent (SGD) optimizer was employed, with the learning rate, momentum, and weight decay set to 0.001, 0.9, and 0.0005, respectively.

In the training process of the MMFM-ML model, to address the issue of sample imbalance, SMOTE oversampling is initially employed, with k_neighbors set to 3. Subsequently, key features are selected based on the relative importance of the features of the random forest model, and the random forest model is then retrained with n_estimators and max_depth set to 340 and 16, respectively.

Our experiments were implemented based on PyTorch, Scikit-learn and run on NVIDIA T4.

3.3 Evaluation Criterion

It is common practice in the field of machine learning to use metrics such as the area under the curve of receiver operating characteristic (AUC-ROC), recall, precision, specificity, and accuracy to assess the performance of classification tasks. In this context, the review score is introduced as a metric to reflect the number of cells that require manual interpretation. The smaller the review score, the fewer cells require manual interpretation. AUC is a performance metric that measures the strengths and weaknesses of the learner, which is defined as the area under the ROC curve that is enclosed with the axes. Other indicators are defined as follows:

$$Recall = \frac{|TP|}{|TP| + |FN|} \tag{1}$$

$$Precision = \frac{|TP|}{|TP| + |FP|} \tag{2}$$

$$Specificity = \frac{|TN|}{|TN| + |FP|} \tag{3}$$

$$Accuracy = \frac{|TN| + |TP|}{|TN| + |TP| + |FN| + |FP|} \tag{4}$$

$$Review\ Score = \frac{|TP| + |FP|}{N_{cell\_seg}} \tag{5}$$

where TP, TN, FP, and FN denote the number of correctly identified CACs, correctly predicted non-CACs, falsely detected CACs, and missed CACs, respectively. N_{cell_seg} denotes the total number of cells resulting from cell segmentation.

3.4 Comparative Experiments

In MMFM-DL network, in order to compare the proposed CACs Patch Partition information fusion with the traditional combine information fusion method, we conducted a test based on Restnet18. The results in Table 1 demonstrate that our proposed CACs Patch Partitioning method outperforms the traditional information fusion method. Furthermore, three backbones, Resnet18 [22], Densent121 [23], and Swin transformer v2, were evaluated in terms of their performance when utilizing CACs Patch Partition information fusion. The results, as presented in Table 2, indicate that Swin transformer v2 exhibited the most favorable outcomes. The table presents AUC of the validation set,

Table 1. The results of testing MMFM-DL network using two multi-channel information fusion methods. Resnet18 (combine) refers to combining a four-color image into one RGB image. Resnet18 (CACs Patch Partition) refers to the proposed method that uses CACs Patch Partition for feature extraction.

Model	Auc	Speed(s)	Total params(M)
Resnet18 (combine)	0.9026	0.015	11.18
Resnet18 (CACs Patch Partition)	0.9237	0.0481	11.38

Table 2. The results of testing MMFM-DL network using three backones.

Model	Auc	Speed(s)	Total params(M)
Resnet18	0.9237	0.0481	11.38
Densenet121	0.9306	0.0671	7.15
swin transformer v2	0.9419	0.0674	27.75

the prediction time per cell (Speed(s)), and the number of model parameters (Total params(M)).

The FISH technique is designed to accurately identify CAC cells from a large number of cells, often tens of thousands. As a result of the nature of FISH samples, which consist primarily of normal cells with very few or no CAC cells, it is critical to address the sample imbalance to ensure the accuracy of the MMFM-ML model. This section compares two methods for addressing the sample imbalance problem: undersampling and oversampling. The process of undersampling involves the removal of a randomly selected portion of samples from normal cells, intending to achieve an equal number of abnormal cells. In contrast, oversampling employs the SMOTE method, as described in Subsect. 2.3. As illustrated in Table 3, the oversampling treatment selects a smaller number of features and exhibits a higher AUC.

Table 3. The results of testing MMFM-ML model using different data imbalance treatment.

Data imbalance treatment	Key features	Cross-validation of AUC
Undersampling	65	0.9524 (0.9046–0.9918)
Oversampling	64	0.9526 (0.9075–0.9915)

3.5 Ablation Study

Ablation experiments were conducted on the baseline, the MMFM-DL network, the MMFM-ML model, and various model fusion strategies, as presented in Table 4. The model performance increases as the number of review cells decreases. Furthermore, the results demonstrate that the model fusion method outperforms both the MMFM-DL network and the MMFM-ML model, with a guaranteed CACs recall rate of 98%. And the MMFM-ML model performs better than the MMFM-DL network. The post-fusion strategy was found to be optimal, followed by the maximum fusion strategy.

Table 4. Ablation study on CACs test set. The baseline only use cell segmentation and signal point detection network. The MMFM-DL model does not employ a fusion strategy and is solely constructed using the deep learning-based model. The MMFM-ML model is constructed solely with the machine learning-based model and does not use a fusion strategy. The MMFM-MDA model uses the mean fusion strategy. The MMFM-MDM model uses the maximum fusion strategy. The MMFM-MDP model uses the post-fusion strategy.

	Recall	Specificity	Accuracy	Precision	Review Score
Baseline	0.99	0.9524	0.9525	0.0213	0.0485
MMFM-DL	0.98	0.3804	0.3933	0.0335	0.0305
MMFM-ML	0.98	0.5973	0.6055	0.0506	0.0202
MMFM-MDA (ML + DL + Avg-fusion)	0.98	0.7326	0.7379	0.0743	0.0137
MMFM-MDM (ML + DL + Max-fusion)	0.98	0.7570	0.7618	0.0812	0.0126
MMFM-MDP (ML + DL + Post-fusion)	**0.98**	**0.8275**	**0.8308**	**0.1107**	**0.0092**

4 Conclusion

Based on the proposed multi-channel multi-model fusion module, we present a method for classifying CAC cells with optimized performance, which could be used for early cancer diagnosis. This method involves feature engineering and constructing a machine-learning model utilizing multi-channel information distribution. Additionally, a deep-learning classification network with multi-channel information fusion is established to provide complementary information. Finally, the information from both models is fused to further enhance the generalization ability of CAC cell classification. This approach effectively reduces the number of cells requiring review while ensuring high CAC cell recall, significantly improving interpretation efficiency.

Experimental results indicate that the MMFM method proposed in this paper increases precision from 2.13% to 11.07% and reduces the Review Score from 485 to 92 per 10,000 cells, implying a significant reduction in review time. However, the method described in this paper involves multiple stages to achieve optimal results, which increases the overall process burden. In the future, we aim to integrate these stages and explore end-to-end CAC cell detection and classification algorithms.

References

1. Poulet, G., Massias, J., Taly, V.: Liquid biopsy: general concepts. Acta Cytol. **63**(6), 449–455 (2019). https://doi.org/10.1159/000499337
2. Katz, R.L., et al.: Genetically abnormal circulating cells in lung cancer patients: an antigen-independent fluorescence in situ hybridization–based case-control study. Clin. Cancer Res.**16**(15), 3976–3987 (2010). https://doi.org/10.1158/1078-0432.CCR-09-3358
3. Katz, R.L., Zaidi, T.M., Pujara, D., et al.: Identification of circulating tumor cells using 4-color fluorescence in situ hybridization: validation of a noninvasive aid for ruling out lung cancer in patients with low-dose computed tomography-detected lung nodules. Cancer: J. American Cancer Society **128**(8), 553–562 (2020)
4. Ye, M., et al.: A classifier for improving early lung cancer diagnosis incorporating artificial intelligence and liquid biopsy. **12**, 677 (2022)
5. Katz, R.L., et al.: Identification of circulating tumor cells using 4-color fluorescence in situ hybridization: validation of a noninvasive aid for ruling out lung cancer in patients with low-dose computed tomography–detected lung nodules. Cancer Cytopathol. **128**(8), 553–562 (2020). https://doi.org/10.1002/cncy.22278
6. Qiu, X., et al.: Application of circulating genetically abnormal cells in the diagnosis of early-stage lung cancer. **148**(3), 685–695 (2022)
7. Liu, W.R., et al.: Detection of circulating genetically abnormal cells in peripheral blood for early diagnosis of non-small cell lung cancer. **11**(11), 3234–3242 (2020)
8. Feng, M., et al.: Detection of circulating genetically abnormal cells using 4-color fluorescence in situ hybridization for the early detection of lung cancer. J. Cancer Res. Clin. Oncol. **147**(8), 2397–2405 (2021). https://doi.org/10.1007/s00432-021-03517-6
9. Yang, H., et al.: Diagnostic value of circulating genetically abnormal cells to support computed tomography for benign and malignant pulmonary nodules. **22**(1), 382 (2022)
10. Feng, M., et al.: Detection of circulating genetically abnormal cells using 4-color fluorescence in situ hybridization for the early detection of lung cancer. J. Cancer Res. Clin. Oncol. **147**(8), 2397–2405 (2021)
11. Xu, C., et al.: An efficient fluorescence in situ hybridization (FISH)-based circulating genetically abnormal cells (CACs) identification method based on Multi-scale MobileNet-YOLO-V4. Quant. Imag. Med. Surg. **12**(5), 2961 (2022)
12. Xu, X., et al.: Attention Mask R-CNN with edge refinement algorithm for identifying circulating genetically abnormal cells. Cytometry A **103**(3), 227–239 (2023)
13. Xu, X., et al.: A lightweight and robust framework for Circulating Genetically Abnormal Cells (CACs) identification using 4-Color Fluorescence In Situ Hybridization (FISH) Image and Deep Refined Learning. J. Digit. Imaging **36**(4), 1687–1700 (2023)
14. Wang, H., Learning, D.-S., with Mean-Teacher Strategy for Circulating Abnormal Cells Identification. CMMCA, et al.: Lecture Notes in Computer Science, vol 14243. Springer, Cham. (2023). https://doi.org/10.1007/978-3-031-45087-7_7
15. Li, X., et al.: Selective Kernel Networks. In: 2019 IEEE/CVF Conference on Computer Vision and Pattern Recognition (CVPR), Long Beach, CA, USA, 2019, pp. 510–519 (2019). https://doi.org/10.1109/CVPR.2019.00060
16. Cao, G., et al.: Feature-fused SSD: fast detection for small objects. In: International Conference on Graphic and Image Processing (2017)

17. Howard A. G., et al.: MobileNets: Efficient Convolutional Neural Networks for Mobile Vision Applications (2017). https://doi.org/10.48550/arXiv.1704.04861
18. Chollet, F.: Xception: Deep Learning with Depthwise Separable Convolutions. In: 2017 IEEE Conference on Computer Vision and Pattern Recognition (CVPR), Honolulu, HI, USA, 2017, pp. 1800–1807 (2017). https://doi.org/10.1109/CVPR.2017.195
19. Liu, Z., et al.: Swin transformer: hierarchical vision transformer using shifted windows. In: 2021 IEEE/CVF International Conference on Computer Vision (ICCV), Montreal, QC, Canada, 2021, pp. 9992–10002 (2021). https://doi.org/10.1109/ICCV48922.2021.00986
20. Liu, Z., et al., Swin transformer v2: scaling up capacity and resolution. In: 2022 IEEE/CVF Conference on Computer Vision and Pattern Recognition (CVPR), New Orleans, LA, USA, 2022, pp. 11999–12009 (2022). https://doi.org/10.1109/CVPR52688.2022.01170
21. Chawla, N.V., Bowyer, K.W., Hall, L.O., Kegelmeyer, W.P.: SMOTE: synthetic minority over-sampling technique. J. Artif. Intell. Res.Intell. Res. **16**, 321–357 (2002). https://doi.org/10.1613/jair.953
22. He, K., et al.: Deep residual learning for image recognition. In: 2016 IEEE Conference on Computer Vision and Pattern Recognition (CVPR), Las Vegas, NV, USA, 2016, pp. 770–778 (2016). https://doi.org/10.1109/CVPR.2016.90
23. Huang, G., et al.: Densely connected convolutional networks. In: 2017 IEEE Conference on Computer Vision and Pattern Recognition (CVPR), Honolulu, HI, USA, 2017, pp. 2261–2269 (2017). https://doi.org/10.1109/CVPR.2017.243

Domain Game: Disentangle Anatomical Feature for Single Domain Generalized Segmentation

Hao Chen[1], Hongrun Zhang[1], U. Wang Chan[2], Rui Yin[3], Xiaofei Wang[1], and Chao Li[1(✉)]

[1] University of Cambridge, Cambridge, UK
cl647@cam.ac.uk
[2] University of Macau, Zhuhai, China
[3] Nanjing Medical University, Nanjing, China

Abstract. Single domain generalization aims to address the challenge of out-of-distribution generalization problem with only one source domain available. Feature disentanglement is a classic solution to this purpose, where the extracted task-related feature is presumed to be resilient to domain shift. However, the absence of references from other domains in a single-domain scenario poses significant uncertainty in feature disentanglement (*ill-posedness*). In this paper, we propose a new framework, named *Domain Game*, to perform feature disentangling for medical image segmentation, based on the observation that anatomical features are more sensitive to geometric transformations, whilst domain-specific features probably will remain invariant to such operations. Results from cross-site test domain evaluation showcase approximately an ~11.8% performance boost in prostate segmentation and around ~10.5% in brain tumor segmentation. The codes will be available at https://github.com/chqwer2/Domain-Game.

Keywords: Generalization · Segmentation · Feature disentanglement

1 Introduction

Background: *Medical image segmentation* serves to classify anatomical structures [11] within organs or lesions at the pixel level. Despite documented success across various applications, significant challenges remain, where segmentation models may fail catastrophically when presented with out-of-distribution data. This challenge is commonly referred to as *domain shift* [14], stemming from variations of intensity distribution across datasets acquired from different protocols or procedures at multiple clinical centers [10].

In this study, we examine a practical but challenging scenario in addressing *domain shift*, attributed to its constrained availability of a single domain (source) for training. This scenario, commonly known as single-domain generalization (SDG) [22], aims to improve generalization capabilities towards multiple novel domains (target). Contrary to the multi-domain approaches that can leverage

© The Author(s), under exclusive license to Springer Nature Switzerland AG 2025
J. Wu et al. (Eds.): CMMCA 2024, LNCS 15181, pp. 41–51, 2025.
https://doi.org/10.1007/978-3-031-73360-4_5

the similarities/variations between different domains, SDG lacks the essential contrastive information to guide the learning process, thus posing challenges in attaining robust generalization across domains.

Related Work: Studies concerning the SDG challenge can be generally categorized into two groups that focus on either data or features. Data-based approaches aim to bridge diverse domains or enhance training diversity through data augmentation or generation [22,26,27]. For instance, *Ouyang et al.* [22] utilize a randomized network functioning as a style generator to develop artificial domains tailored specifically for training from a single source. Despite being effective in managing minor distribution changes, data-based approaches are vulnerable to substantial domain shifts beyond their training strategy.

Feature-based methods are designed to utilize domain-invariant features to enhance model resilience against unforeseen out-of-domain influences [7,24]. Central to feature-based approaches is the feasibility of distinguishing domain-invariant features (X) from domain-specific features (Δ) within an intricate high-dimensional feature space $(E(I))$ derived from a given image I:

$$E(I) = X \oplus (\Delta), \tag{1}$$

where $E(\cdot)$ signifies a mapping function that transforms an image into its representation within feature space and $\oplus$ denotes the feature fusion operation.

It is of note that surrounding Δ with parentheses indicates that in some methodologies [18,29,30], the domain-specific features are not explicitly delineated. For instance, the *feature alignment* approach [29,30] serves as an efficient strategy for aligning the distributions of X across source and target domains, thereby mitigating the domain discrepancies. Similarly, the *domain shifts with uncertainty* (DSU) [18] integrates feature statistics for modeling the uncertainty of X through analyzing multiple augmented examples, aiming to alleviate the model uncertainty on the target domain. However, these methods are challenged by the ill-posed nature[1] emphasized by Eq. 1, rendering isolating only X insufficient for ensuring its consistency across domains.

In response to the ill-posed challenge, *feature disentanglement* offers an alternative approach that explicitly models X and Δ and then distinguishes them [4,21]. For example, a recent endeavor [8] proposes that Δ conforms to a normal distribution, wherein $\Delta \in \mathcal{N}(\mu, \text{diag}(\sigma)^{-1})$, with both μ and σ being trainable parameters. By holding Δ constant, Eq. 1 turns deterministic. However, the Gaussian prior assumption imposes strict constraints on the underlying distribution, which may not effectively capture the complex and varied nature of the *domain shift*, potentially leading to oversimplified representations [15]. It is worthnoted that *Gu et al.* [9] propose a disentangle framework that utilize style augmentation to generates image with same pathology structure but in different style to separate domain-agnostic X. While we observe that the domain shift may not just the intensity distribution that relates to the machine, but also has population-specific shift that may affect the distribution of the autonomic feature, *e.g.* patients from different continent or in different age groups. Drawing

---

[1] This denotes the existence of more than one possible solution to the equation.

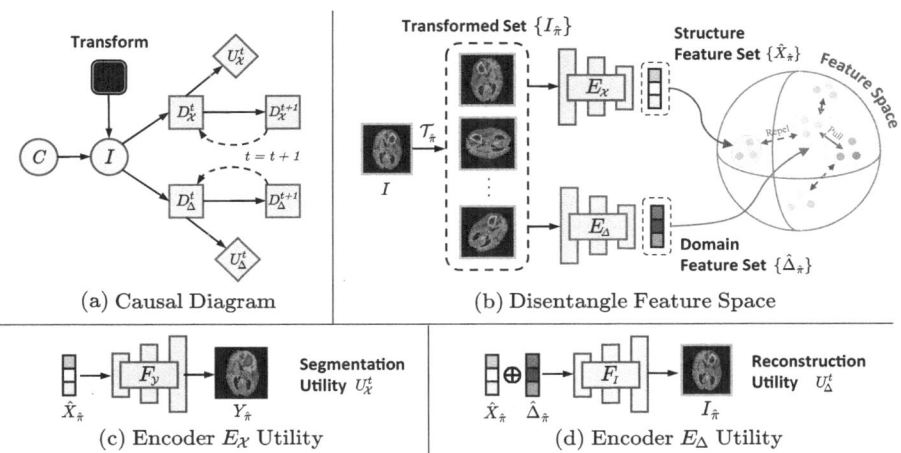

(a) Causal Diagram

(b) Disentangle Feature Space

(c) Encoder $E_\mathcal{X}$ Utility

(d) Encoder E_Δ Utility

Fig. 1. Domain Game Overview. Colours indicates the relation to distinct features, *i.e.* purple - overall, red - anatomical and blue - domain-specific features. (a) Image I is drawn from singular domain (C) to update the parameters D at each step according to utilities U. (b) Transformed set is generated by applying $\mathcal{T}_{\hat{\pi}}$ to I, and subsequently encoded into feature sets by two encoders. Then features within $\{\hat{\Delta}_{\hat{\pi}}\}$ are pull together to learn domain-specific character and introduce repulsion between $\{\hat{X}_{\hat{\pi}}\}$ and $\{\hat{\Delta}_{\hat{\pi}}\}$ to enforce disentanglement. (c) The quality of $\hat{X}_{\hat{\pi}}$ is measured through segmentation utility. (d) The disentanglement is achieved by fusing randomly paired $\hat{X}$ and $\hat{\Delta}$ to reconstruct the input.

from this attention, we propose in this paper to learn the diagnostic feature in the highlight learning process on the by interference of X to learn to extract the X from images samples have different X but share same domain Δ, thus more focus on the autonomy structure distribution.

Motivation and Contributions: Following the aforementioned analysis, we seek to develop a feature disentanglement method that does not rely on explicit assumptions about the underlying distributions of either X or Δ. Clinically, the *anatomical features* of organs or lesions (*e.g.* mass tumors) are consistently associated with local anatomical structures across domains, *i.e.* domain-invariant features. However, we observe that these structural intricacies in a specific image are responsive to geometric transformations; *e.g.* rotating an image will also rotate its geometric information. Conversely, the *domain-specific features* are more associated with the overall intensity distribution. Given that transformations do not alter this distribution, domain-specific features remain unaffected by geometric transformations.

In this paper, we introduce a novel feature disentanglement framework within a single domain. We elucidate this framework using an analogy to combinatorial games to leverage the distinct feature characteristics, thereby introducing our concept called the *Domain Game*. The contributions of this work are threefold:

Algorithm 1. Domain Game

Require: paired set $\{I, Y\}_{\text{set}}$, iterations N, transform $\mathcal{T}_{\hat{\pi}}$
    initialize encoders $E_{\mathcal{X}}^t$ and E_{Δ}^t and decoder functions $F_{\mathcal{Y}}^t$ and F_I^t
    while $N \neq 0$ **do**
        sample $I, Y \in \{I, Y\}$
        apply $\{I_{\hat{\pi}}\} \leftarrow \mathcal{T}_{\hat{\pi}}(I)$, $\{Y_{\hat{\pi}}\} \leftarrow \mathcal{T}_{\hat{\pi}}(Y)$ ▷ geometric transformation
        get features iteratively, loop every $I_{\hat{\pi}} \in \{I_{\hat{\pi}}\}$
            $\hat{X}_{\hat{\pi}} \leftarrow E_{\mathcal{X}}^t(I_{\hat{\pi}})$, $\hat{\Delta}_{\hat{\pi}} \leftarrow E_{\Delta}^t(I_{\hat{\pi}})$
        calculate $\mathcal{L}_{\mathcal{FD}}$ ▷ *Step 1* feature disentanglement
        Updates Encoder $E_{\mathcal{X}}^t$ parameters:
            get $\hat{Y}_{\hat{\pi}} \leftarrow F_{\mathcal{Y}}^t(\hat{X}_{\hat{\pi}})$
            calculate $U_{\mathcal{X}}^t \leftarrow \text{Dice}(Y_{\hat{\pi}}, \hat{Y}_{\hat{\pi}})$ ▷ *Step 2* segmentation utility
        Updates Encoder E_{Δ}^t parameters:
            get $\hat{I}_{\hat{\pi}} \leftarrow F_I^t(\hat{\Delta}_s | \hat{X}_{\hat{\pi}})$, Δ_s sampled from $\{\hat{\Delta}_{\hat{\pi}}\}$
            calculate $U_{\Delta}^t \leftarrow \text{PSNR}(I_{\hat{\pi}}, \hat{I}_{\hat{\pi}})$ ▷ *Step 2* reconstruction utility
        $N \leftarrow N - 1$
    end while

- We propose *Domain Game*, a new paradigm in single-domain generalization that seeks to address the inherent ill-posed challenge of feature disentanglement by leveraging our prior knowledge of diagnostic feature characteristics.
- To emphasize the distinct feature properties for facilitating disentanglement, the *Domain Game* introduces these properties as update utilities specific to different networks. Intriguingly, two networks strategically intertwine to disentangle the feature space, reflecting an analogy with combinatorial games.
- We perform extensive experiments and validate that the proposed method effectively produces more robust features and outperforms state-of-the-art models on out-of-distribution test domains.

2 Methodology

Figure 1a illustrates the overview causal diagram of the *Domain Game*. The context variables (C) symbolize the single domain where the image (I) is sampled at each iteration step. As indicated in Fig. 1b, *Domain Game* introduces two encoders $(E_{\mathcal{X}}^t, E_{\Delta}^t)$ to learn the disentangled feature sets. The parameters $(D,$ squares) and utility variables $(U,$ diamonds) associated with these encoders are indicated by the same color. For each iteration, both encoders compute their utility functions U^t based on the current parameter D^t and evolve to an optimized parameter D^{t+1} in the next iteration $(t + 1)$. The algorithmic flow of Domain-Game is illustrated in Algorithm 1, and we will introduce its key steps in the following sections.

***Step 1.* Feature Disentanglement.** Conventional feature learning typically focuses on establishing a direct one-to-one mapping between images and corresponding features, denoted as $I \rightarrow X$. While it is straightforward, the amalgamation of diverse image aspects into a singular feature frequently poses challenges for models to effectively operate across varied domains.

To address this constraint, we propose to separate the anatomical features crucial for the diagnostic process from the domain features inherent in the captured image properties. Our clinical observations reveal that the geometry description is prominent in describing anatomical structures, *e.g.* shape, size, orientation, and spatial relationships. Thus, the local anatomical features are responsive to geometric alterations, *i.e.* geometry transformations will alter the structures, resulting in distinctive features. On the other hand, the imaging property (ref as domain feature in medical images) maintains its integrity when subjected to geometric transformations.

Specifically, we employ a multitude of viewpoints through diverse randomly transformed instances to offer a unique estimation for features that exhibit within ill-posed nature. At each interaction, a set of n geometric transformations denoted as $\{\mathcal{T}_{\hat{\pi}_i}\}$ is stochastically sampled, where $\hat{\pi}$ signifies the transformed effect, and $i \in \mathbb{N} : 0 < i \leq n$ represents the index. Subsequently, every transformation $\mathcal{T}_{\hat{\pi}_i}$ is applied to the image-label pair (I, Y), generating the transformed pair $(I_{\hat{\pi}_i}, Y_{\hat{\pi}_i})$. The encoders then derive $\hat{X}_{\hat{\pi}_i}$ and $\hat{\Delta}_{\hat{\pi}_i}$ from the input $I_{\hat{\pi}_i}$ based on current parameters set D^t, as illustrated in Fig. 1a:

$$\mathcal{L}_{\mathcal{FD}} = \sum_i^n \left\| \mathcal{T}_{\hat{\pi}_i}(\hat{X}) - \hat{X}_{\hat{\pi}_i} \right\|^2 + \sum_i^n \sum_{j \neq i}^n \left\| \hat{\Delta}_{\hat{\pi}_j} - \hat{\Delta}_{\hat{\pi}_i} \right\|^2. \tag{2}$$

Within this framework, the symbol $\hat{X}$ signifies the anatomical feature from the unaltered input I. To ensure consistent alignment between anatomical structures, it undergoes a congruent transformation denoted as $\mathcal{T}_{\hat{\pi}}$, in accordance with $I_{\hat{\pi}_i}$. The transformation $\mathcal{T}_{\hat{\pi}}$ acts on the spatial dimensions represented by $\mathbb{R}^{H \times W}$ within the input $\hat{X}$, which is structured as $\mathbb{R}^{C \times H \times W}$.

***Step 2*. Posterior Utility Maximisation.** The anatomical features $\hat{X}_{\hat{\pi}}$ produced by the encoder $E_{\mathcal{X}}^t$ are utilized by the decoder function $F_y^t(\cdot)$ for segmentation purposes. The performance of this segmentation process is assessed using the Dice coefficient, which quantifies the utility as:

$$U_{\mathcal{X}}^t = \text{Dice}(F_y^t(\hat{X}_{\hat{\pi}}), Y_{\hat{\pi}}). \tag{3}$$

Encoder E_{Δ}^t aims to isolate domain features that are not exclusively tied to a particular image. This is achieved by randomly sampling a $\hat{\Delta}_s \in \{\hat{\Delta}_{\hat{\pi}}\}$ and pairing it with a $\hat{X}_{\hat{\pi}}$ to reconstruct the $I_{\hat{\pi}}$ using the decoder $F_I^t(\cdot)$. Given that $\hat{X}_{\hat{\pi}}$ is associated with a specific $I_{\hat{\pi}}$ while $\hat{\Delta}_s$ is not, $\hat{X}_{\hat{\pi}}$ serves as the condition for specifying the reconstruction target. The utility of E_{Δ}^t can be assessed by the reconstruction fidelity using the Peak Signal-to-Noise Ratio (PSNR):

$$U_{\Delta}^t = \text{PSNR}(I_{\hat{\pi}}, F_I^t(\hat{\Delta}_s | \hat{X}_{\hat{\pi}})), \ \hat{\Delta}_s \in \{\hat{\Delta}_{\hat{\pi}}\}. \tag{4}$$

2.1   Implementing Details

This segment delineates the network architecture specifics and training approach for the *Domain Game*. Two encoders are represented by EfficientNet-B2 [25], following the setting of BayeSeg [8]. The decoder functions employ DeeplabV3 [5] for segmentation or reconstruction inference. The optimization utilizes the AdamW optimizer with a learning rate set to 1e−4 for 1200 epochs. The learning rate decay adheres to a CosineAnnealing [20] with a time span of 30 units.

We employ lasso penalty on the feature space to eliminate redundant dimensions, thereby effectively imposing shrinkage on less meaningful space [31].

$$\mathcal{L}_{\text{Lasso}} = \|\hat{X} + \hat{\Delta}\|, \tag{5}$$

where $\hat{X} = E_{\chi}^t(I)$ and $\hat{\Delta} = E_{\Delta}^t(I)$ are derived based on current parameters D_{χ}^t and D_{Δ}^t, correspondingly, at iteration t.

The optimization process is conducted across the entirety of the *Domain-Game*, utilizing a *minmax* strategy to minimize the loss associated with constraining the features, while simultaneously maximizing the utility functions for segmentation or reconstruction. This optimization formula can be expressed as:

$$\arg_{D_{\chi}^t, D_{\Delta}^t, P_{y}^t, P_{I}^t} \min_{\mathcal{L}} \max_{U} (\lambda\mathcal{L}_{\mathcal{FD}}) - (U_{\chi}^t + \omega U_{\Delta}^t), \tag{6}$$

where the norm weight, denoted as λ and ω, determined as $\lambda = 5$ and $\omega = 5e^{-2}$ through experimentation to balance between feature redundancy and an overly simplified space, and stabilize learning utilities.

3 Experiments

3.1 Experimental Setup

We evaluate our proposed method on two different tasks, including 1) the Prostate segmentation task and 2) the Brain tumor segmentation task. We compare four state-of-the-art approaches for domain generalization, *i.e.* Cutout [6], IBN-Net [23], RandConv [28], DSU [18], and BayeSeg [8]. EfficientNet-B2 [25] is used as the backbone for all methods and train for 1200 epochs for a fair comparison. In each source dataset, the data is randomly divided into training (70%), validation (10%), and testing (20%). The model achieving the best performance on the source test set is chosen for the target domain evaluation.
Note: The quantitative metrics for segmentation include the Dice coefficient and Jaccard similarity scores, reported on a scale of $10e−2$.

3.2 Prostate Segmentation

Prostate segmentation benefits accurate volume measurement and boundary estimation, which aids diagnostic procedures for prostate diseases [19]. We employ three public MRI datasets: NCI-ISBI 2013 [3] (n = 60), I2CVB [16] (n = 19), and PROMISE12 [19] (n = 37). The patient number of each dataset is denoted by n. The datasets are split into six domains depending on the medical centres from which they originate (RUNMC, BMC, I2CVB, UCL, BIDMC, and HK).

Table 1. Prostate segmentation performance across diverse target sites. The Dice score is reported in mean±std. The red down-arrow number indicates declined performance from source to target and lower values shows better generalization.

Method	(Source)	(Cross-site Target)					Avg. on Target
	RUNMC [3]	BMC [3]	BIDMC [19]	HK [19]	UCL [19]	I2CVB [16]	
Cutout [6]	85.88 ± 04.2	79.42 ± 06.9	54.42 ± 13.3	77.17 ± 06.8	79.75 ± 03.2	78.99 ± 06.2	73.95 (↓11.9)
IBN-Net [23]	86.13 ± 05.5	78.04 ± 07.1	43.41 ± 20.1	75.81 ± 06.0	79.39 ± 04.1	79.44 ± 06.2	71.22 (↓14.9)
RandConv [28]	**87.68 ± 04.4**	83.75 ± 05.0	54.35 ± 15.8	77.89 ± 06.4	83.76 ± 05.1	77.21 ± 12.3	75.39 (↓12.3)
DSU [18]	85.49 ± 07.2	77.89 ± 06.1	66.14 ± 12.5	75.77 ± 07.4	78.49 ± 04.1	75.89 ± 12.8	74.84 (↓10.7)
BayeSeg [8]	86.57 ± 05.7	81.82 ± 06.9	66.56 ± 17.8	80.62 ± 05.3	81.25 ± 06.6	77.52 ± 17.1	77.52 (↓09.1)
Domain Game	86.92 ± 05.3	**85.42 ± 05.4**	**75.79 ± 13.1**	**84.33 ± 05.5**	**86.10 ± 04.5**	**79.50 ± 05.2**	**82.23 (↓ 04.7)**

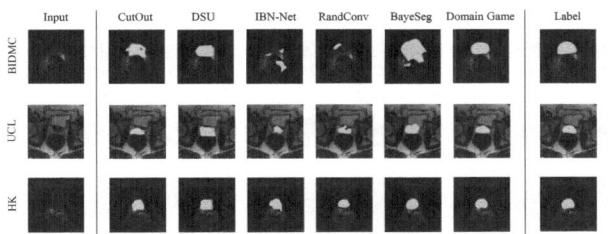 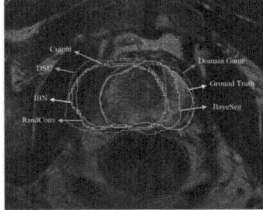

(a) Visualization for cross-site prostate segmentation.   (b) Detailed comparison.

Fig. 2. Qualitative visualization through (a) broad and (b) intricate comparisons.

Analysis: In Table 1, RandConv [28] attains the highest dice in the source domain, while Domain Game reaches the smallest average performance drop at around ˜5.4% in the target domains. Notably, the BIDMC dataset exhibits a significant performance decline compared to other target datasets, possibly impacted by its bias fields. In this context, our approach surpasses the second-best performance achieved by BayeSeg by approximately ˜11.8%.

Figure 2a presents the qualitative segmentation results. Notably, DSU and Domain Game consistently deliver satisfactory outcomes, with Domain Game more resembling the labels. Figure 2b presents a comprehensive comparative analysis within an example of the UCL domain. The results reveal that all the methods other than Domain Game exhibit a leftward bias, while Domain Game notably preserves a closer alignment to the ground-truth label.

3.3   Brain Tumor Segmentation

We aim to validate our method through brain tumor segmentation [17] and investigate its utility across diverse geographic regions and age groups.

We choose three datasets in this task, with Brats-Glioma [2] ($n = 1251$) as source domain, Brats-Africa [1] ($n = 60$) and BraTS-PEDs [13] ($n = 228$) as target domains. Data from Brats-Glioma [2] patients were collected using various protocols and scanners across multiple institutions. The Brats-Africa [1] comprises data with unique characteristics, with low image contrast and resolution

Table 2. Brain tumor segmentation results reported in Dice and Jaccard scores.

Method	(Source) BraTS-Glioma [2]		(Cross-site Target) BraTS-Africa [1]		(Cross-age Target) BraTS-Pediatrics [13]		Avg. on Target	
	Dice	Jaccard	Dice	Jaccard	Dice	Jaccard	Dice	Jaccard
Cutout [6]	75.78 ± 14.2	72.19 ± 25.3	57.37 ± 27.0	54.82 ± 23.8	45.57 ± 22.2	39.16 ± 18.2	51.47 (↓24.31)	46.99 (↓25.20)
IBN-Net [23]	77.94 ± 17.3	73.92 ± 27.2	62.31 ± 26.5	51.75 ± 20.6	54.46 ± 22.4	42.03 ± 20.3	58.39 (↓19.55)	46.89 (↓27.03)
RandConv [28]	**81.38 ± 12.2**	**76.98 ± 25.2**	63.35 ± 29.1	53.18 ± 23.4	51.83 ± 24.9	50.69 ± 19.7	57.59 (↓23.79)	51.94 (↓25.05)
DSU [18]	79.23 ± 14.6	75.31 ± 26.4	61.09 ± 28.7	52.62 ± 24.9	55.12 ± 21.5	52.78 ± 19.6	58.11 (↓21.12)	52.70 (↓22.61)
BayeSeg [8]	78.28 ± 17.6	74.83 ± 28.5	62.88 ± 27.5	56.83 ± 22.5	51.89 ± 21.7	51.65 ± 16.1	57.39 (↓20.89)	54.24 (↓20.59)
Domain-Game	78.47 ± 17.3	75.49 ± 29.1	**69.73 ± 26.3**	**62.05 ± 28.5**	**60.36 ± 22.6**	**57.02 ± 17.2**	**65.05 (↓ 13.42)**	**59.53 (↓ 15.95)**

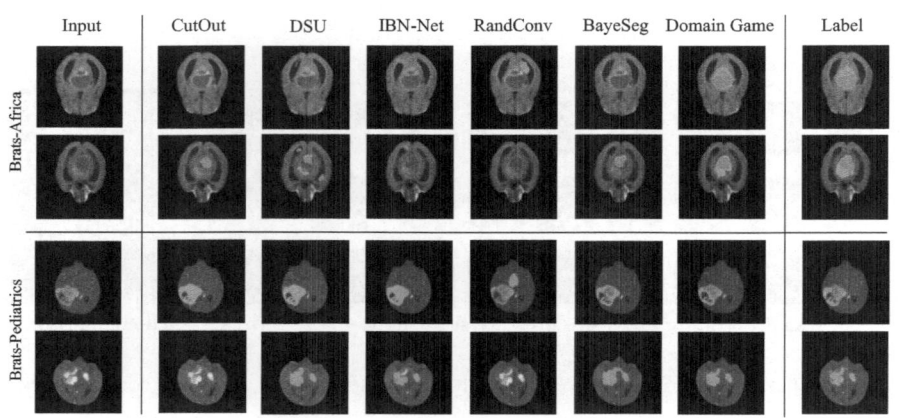

Fig. 3. Qualitative visualization of brain tumor segmentation.

due to lower-quality MRI technology in areas surrounding Sub-Saharan Africa. BraTS-Pediatrics [13] assembles pediatric brain tumor patients characterized by differing imaging and clinical profiles compared to adult brain tumors.

We specifically select the post-gadolinium T1-weighted (T1Gd) sequence for our experiments as it is frequently utilized in clinical practice for delineating tumor morphology. We chose to classify the enhancing tumors (ET) and the non-enhancing tumor core (NTC) as these two labels are annotated in both the Brats-Glioma and Brats-Africa datasets. However, we only assessed ET in Brats-Pediatrics as it exclusively includes ET [13].

Analysis: Table 2 presents the Dice and Jaccard scores. In summary, Domain Game achieves the highest average scores in both metrics on target domains, at *65.05* and *59.53*, respectively. This signifies an approximate ˜*10.5%* boost in Dice compared to the second-best score achieved by IBN-Net [23], and around ˜*8.6%* increase in Jaccard score surpassing the second-best BayeSeg [8].

We showcase some qualitative visualizations of brain tumor segmentation results in Fig. 3. Existing model frequently face challenges in diagnosing diseases across diverse geographical regions, age groups and tumor subtypes. We aim to achieve a model with robust domain generalization capabilities, which, when extensively trained only with single resource, helps address these issues in fields where have insufficient imaging data for training [12].

4 Conclusion

We propose a new framework to tackle the domain shift when only one source domain is available, in which an efficient mechanism is exquisitely designed to disentangle anatomical and domain-specific features, respectively. The new method is motivated by the observation of the distinct responses of these two features to geometric transformations. Experimental results demonstrate the effectiveness and efficiency of the proposed method in improving the generalizability of a trained model to wider domains. We expect the proposed method can serve as a useful tool to alleviate the ubiquitous domain shift problem in real-world clinical applications.

References

1. Adewole, M., et al.: The brain tumor segmentation (BraTS) challenge 2023: glioma segmentation in Sub-Saharan Africa patient population (BraTS-Africa). ArXiv (2023)
2. Baid, U., et al.: The RSNA-ASNR-MICCAI BraTS 2021 benchmark on brain tumor segmentation and radiogenomic classification. arXiv preprint arXiv:2107.02314 (2021)
3. Bloch, N., et al.: NCI-ISBI 2013 challenge: automated segmentation of prostate structures. Comput. Biol. Med. (2021)
4. Chen, H., Qu, C., Zhang, Y., Chen, C., Jiao, J.: Multi-view self-supervised disentanglement for general image denoising. In: Proceedings of the IEEE/CVF International Conference on Computer Vision, pp. 12281–12291 (2023)
5. Chen, L.-C., Zhu, Y., Papandreou, G., Schroff, F., Adam, H.: Encoder-decoder with atrous separable convolution for semantic image segmentation. In: Ferrari, V., Hebert, M., Sminchisescu, C., Weiss, Y. (eds.) ECCV 2018. LNCS, vol. 11211, pp. 833–851. Springer, Cham (2018). https://doi.org/10.1007/978-3-030-01234-2_49
6. DeVries, T., Taylor, G.W.: Improved regularization of convolutional neural networks with cutout. arXiv preprint arXiv:1708.04552 (2017)
7. Dou, Q., Coelho de Castro, D., Kamnitsas, K., Glocker, B.: Domain generalization via model-agnostic learning of semantic features. In: Advances in Neural Information Processing Systems, vol. 32 (2019)
8. Gao, S., Zhou, H., Gao, Y., Zhuang, X.: BayeSeg: Bayesian modeling for medical image segmentation with interpretable generalizability. Med. Image Anal. **89**, 102889 (2023). https://doi.org/10.1016/J.MEDIA.2023.102889
9. Gu, R., et al.: CDDSA: contrastive domain disentanglement and style augmentation for generalizable medical image segmentation. Med. Image Anal. **89**, 102904 (2023)
10. Guan, H., Liu, M.: Domain adaptation for medical image analysis: a survey. IEEE Trans. Biomed. Eng. **69**(3), 1173–1185 (2021)
11. Hussain, S., et al.: Modern diagnostic imaging technique applications and risk factors in the medical field: a review. BioMed Res. Int. **2022** (2022)

12. Jha, S., Topol, E.J.: Upending the model of AI adoption. Lancet **401**(10392), 1920 (2023)
13. Kazerooni, A.F., et al.: The brain tumor segmentation (BraTS) challenge 2023: focus on pediatrics (CBTN-CONNECT-DIPGR-ASNR-MICCAI BraTS-PEDs). ArXiv (2023)
14. Kondrateva, E., Pominova, M., Popova, E., Sharaev, M., Bernstein, A., Burnaev, E.: Domain shift in computer vision models for MRI data analysis: an overview. In: Thirteenth International Conference on Machine Vision, vol. 11605, pp. 126–133. SPIE (2021)
15. Landry, D., Pomerleau, F., Giguere, P.: Cello-3D: estimating the covariance of ICP in the real world. In: 2019 International Conference on Robotics and Automation (ICRA), pp. 8190–8196. IEEE (2019)
16. Lemaître, G., Martí, R., Freixenet, J., Vilanova, J.C., Walker, P.M., Meriaudeau, F.: Computer-aided detection and diagnosis for prostate cancer based on mono and multi-parametric MRI: a review. Comput. Biol. Med. **60**, 8–31 (2015)
17. Li, C., et al.: Expectation-maximization regularised deep learning for tumour segmentation. In: Proceedings - International Symposium on Biomedical Imaging, April 2023. https://doi.org/10.1109/ISBI53787.2023.10230573
18. Li, X., Dai, Y., Ge, Y., Liu, J., Shan, Y., Duan, L.Y.: Uncertainty modeling for out-of-distribution generalization. arXiv preprint arXiv:2202.03958 (2022)
19. Litjens, G., et al.: Evaluation of prostate segmentation algorithms for MRI: the promise12 challenge. Med. Image Anal. **18**(2), 359–373 (2014)
20. Loshchilov, I., Hutter, F.: SGDR: stochastic gradient descent with warm restarts. arXiv preprint arXiv:1608.03983 (2016)
21. Mao, Y., Jiang, L., Chen, X., Li, C.: DisC-Diff: disentangled conditional diffusion model for multi-contrast MRI super-resolution. In: Greenspan, H., et al. (eds.) MICCAI 2023. LNCS, vol. 14229, pp. 387–397. Springer, Cham (2023). https://doi.org/10.1007/978-3-031-43999-5_37. https://arxiv.org/abs/2303.13933v2
22. Ouyang, C., et al.: Causality-inspired single-source domain generalization for medical image segmentation. IEEE Trans. Med. Imaging **42**(4), 1095–1106 (2022)
23. Pan, X., Luo, P., Shi, J., Tang, X.: Two at once: enhancing learning and generalization capacities via IBN-Net. In: Ferrari, V., Hebert, M., Sminchisescu, C., Weiss, Y. (eds.) ECCV 2018. LNCS, vol. 11208, pp. 484–500. Springer, Cham (2018). https://doi.org/10.1007/978-3-030-01225-0_29
24. Sun, X., et al.: Recovering latent causal factor for generalization to distributional shifts. In: Advances in Neural Information Processing Systems, vol. 34, pp. 16846–16859 (2021)
25. Tan, M., Le, Q.: EfficientNet: rethinking model scaling for convolutional neural networks. In: International Conference on Machine Learning, pp. 6105–6114. PMLR (2019)
26. Volpi, R., Namkoong, H., Sener, O., Duchi, J.C., Murino, V., Savarese, S.: Generalizing to unseen domains via adversarial data augmentation. In: Advances in Neural Information Processing Systems, vol. 31 (2018)
27. Xu, Y., Xie, S., Reynolds, M., Ragoza, M., Gong, M., Batmanghelich, K.: Adversarial consistency for single domain generalization in medical image segmentation. In: Wang, L., Dou, Q., Fletcher, P.T., Speidel, S., Li, S. (eds.) MICCAI 2022. LNCS, vol. 13437, pp. 671–681. Springer, Cham (2022). https://doi.org/10.1007/978-3-031-16449-1_64
28. Xu, Z., Liu, D., Yang, J., Raffel, C., Niethammer, M.: Robust and generalizable visual representation learning via random convolutions. arXiv preprint arXiv:2007.13003 (2020)

29. Zhao, S., Gong, M., Liu, T., Fu, H., Tao, D.: Domain generalization via entropy regularization. In: Advances in Neural Information Processing Systems, vol. 33, pp. 16096–16107 (2020)
30. Zhao, X., et al.: Robust white matter hyperintensity segmentation on unseen domain. In: 2021 IEEE 18th International Symposium on Biomedical Imaging (ISBI), pp. 1047–1051. IEEE (2021)
31. Zhu, Z., et al.: A geometric analysis of neural collapse with unconstrained features. In: Advances in Neural Information Processing Systems, vol. 34, pp. 29820–29834 (2021)

Attention-Fusion Model for Multi-omics (AMMO) Data Integration in Lung Adenocarcinoma

Wentao Li[1,2] (ID), Amgad Muneer[1] (ID), Muhammad Waqas[1] (ID), Xiaobo Zhou[2] (ID), and Jia Wu[1(✉)] (ID)

[1] Department of Imaging Physics, The University of Texas MD Anderson Cancer Center, Houston, TX 77030, USA
jwu11@mdanderson.org
[2] McWilliams School of Biomedical Informatics at UTHealth Houston, Houston, TX 77030, USA

Abstract. The multi-omics integration gives a whole new perspective into pathway analysis to reveal the complicated nature of cellular systems. While the understanding of interactions among different omics data remains unknown, current methods do not consider the unique and similar properties. In this paper, we propose Attention-fusion Model for Multi-Omics (AMMO), a robust method that addresses this challenge through domain separation. Our proposed attention-based approach inherently captures the similarities and differences across various omics modalities, enhancing the interpretability of the integrated data. Our proposed method can achieve a state-of-the-art C-index of 0.8017 in overall survival prediction in TCGA-LUAD data with the diverse types of omics data: DNA Methylation, exon expression RNA Seq (HiC), and protein expression (RPPA). We also demonstrated the performance increase by adding more modalities with the ablation test, the results confirmed our assumption of improving model performance by including more modalities to our method.

Keywords: Multi-omics · Attention model · Single cell

1 Introduction

The recent advancements of biotechnology have enabled the collection of extensive molecular data related to the different biological processes of transcription and translation. This includes data from genomes, transcriptomics, proteomics, and metabolomics [1, 2]. However, focusing on one single modality of these molecular data may not adequately capture the underlying biological relationships among the different layers. Therefore, developing a multi-omics approach is an active area of research [3].

In cancer studies, multi-omics integration can provide several advantages over a single modality, where they can better measure intra-tumor heterogeneity [4], lead to robust biomarker discovery and validation [5], and uncover key regulatory mechanisms [6], among other applications [7]. Different omics modalities often exhibit both common

© The Author(s), under exclusive license to Springer Nature Switzerland AG 2025
J. Wu et al. (Eds.): CMMCA 2024, LNCS 15181, pp. 52–60, 2025.
https://doi.org/10.1007/978-3-031-73360-4_6

and unique patterns in their expression and effects on the human body [8]. For example, genomic data provides insights into genetic predispositions, transcriptomic data provides information on gene expression levels, proteomic data on protein abundance and interactions, and metabolomic data on metabolic changes. These modalities' common or interacting patterns can help identify the biomarker and therapeutic targets. Therefore, combining both unique and similar patterns can offer a comprehensive understanding of cancer system biology [9–12].

The existing multi-omics studies rely on either early or late fusion techniques [13], as shown in Fig. 1. The early fusion approach integrates the data at the early stage of the analysis, this approach extracts combined patterns while preserving the interdependencies among different omics modalities [14]. Late fusion, however, combines individual omics abstracted features as an input to fit an integral model. By treating all data types as a single input, early fusion can potentially exploit the interactions between different omics layers from the outset, providing a more unified analysis [15, 16].

Although these techniques have been adopted by several studies in the literature, these fusion techniques overlook inherent complexities and synergistic interactions in the case of multi-omics datasets and overlook the importance of explicitly capturing both the shared and distinct patterns harbored within different omics data types. For instance, the study by MOPA (Multi-Omics Pathway Analysis) integrates multi-omics data. Still, it primarily focuses on gene-centric pathways, potentially missing the broader context provided by integrating proteomic and metabolomic data [17]. Similarly, the integrative analysis using directed random walks for survival prediction [18] focuses on gene expression and copy number alterations but fails to consider the unique contributions of proteomics and metabolomics, which can reveal distinct and complementary biological insights [18]. By neglecting these patterns, traditional methods may not fully exploit the potential of multi-omics data to uncover intricate biological interactions and disease pathways, leading to incomplete or biased interpretations of biological systems.

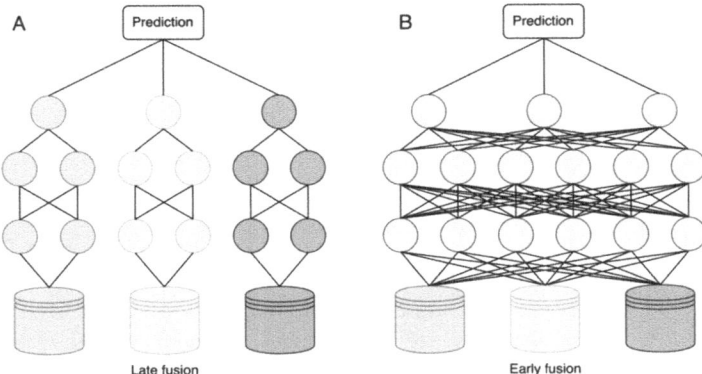

Fig. 1. Two main types of data fusion approaches. The color manifests different types of omics modalities. A) Late fusion, which may lose shared similarities representations; B) Early fusion, which may lose unique representations.

To address the challenge of extracting and combining unique and shared patterns in multi-omics data at the same time, we proposed an end-to-end trainable attention-based mixed-fusion approach. The proposed approach extracts unique and common patterns from different omics modalities and fuses them to obtain improved analysis performance. The proposed approach weighs on collecting both synergistic relationships and channel-specific insights, thus boosting model resilience and interpretation, allowing the discovery of new knowledge on complex system biology.

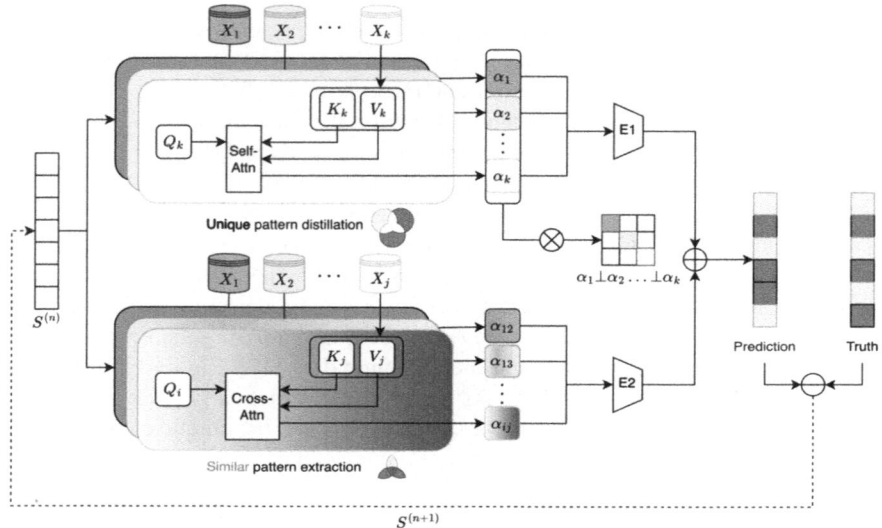

Fig. 2. Flowchart of Attention-fusion Model for Multi-Omics (AMMO). The proposed method uses self-attentional modules and cross-attentional modules to extract both unique and similar patterns from the multi-omics modalities. The shared similarity latency will be updated throughout the iterations. The similar pattern extraction computes the cross-attention from pair-wise modalities i and j.

2 Methods

Before we elaborate on our model, let's define some notations. Assume there are k different types of omics data, and denote $X_i \in \mathcal{R}^{N \times p_i}$ as the omic data from modality $i \in [1, 2, \ldots, k]$, where p_i is the feature dimension of the omics modality, N is sample number, and θ is the parameters space of the model. K_i and V_i denote as the Key and Value representation matrices of an attention-based module and can be derived from assigned weights W_i^k and W_i^v, namely $K_i = W_i^k X_i$ and $V_i = W_i^v X_i$. Since our method aims to distill the common patterns across modalities and capture the pattern, we define S as the shared representation latency that is shared across different modalities. Notice that S will be updated throughout the learning iterations, for further detailed annotation in step n, we denote it as $S^{(n)}$. Finally, Q_i denotes as the Query representation latency vector derived from shared representation latency $S^{(n)}$, derived from $Q_i = W_i^q S^{(n)}$. For each omics modality i:

1. Query representation: $Q_i = W_i^q S^{(n)}$
2. Key representation: $K_i = W_i^k X_i$
3. Value representation: $V_i = W_i^v X_i$

2.1 Model Architecture of AMMO

The schematic representation of our proposed model is shown in Fig. 2. The model will start with an initial shared similarity latency, which contains mixed unseparated modality information. Then this latency will enter two modules at the same time, similar pattern extraction and unique pattern distillation. The unique pattern distillation module consists of multi-head self-attention and forces the attention outcome α_i to be orthogonal across different channels, this process will learn and capture the unique patterns within the multi-head self-attention module. Meanwhile, the similar pattern extraction module feeds the shared similarity latency to multi-head cross-attention layers and learns the shared information among different modalities pair-wisely. Then, both unique patterns and similar patterns are fed through linear encoders $E1$ and $E2$, this will map the two latencies into the same dimension.

2.2 Extracting the Similarity

To extract the shared information among different omics modalities, we designed a pair-wise cross-attention module. This module aims to distill the common patterns across modalities and capture these patterns pair-wisely. To calculate the cross-attention, we use the scaled dot-product attention mechanism. The cross-attention score α_{ij} is computed as follows:

$$\alpha_{ij}\left(S^{(n)}, X_i, X_j; \theta\right) = Attention\left(Q_j, K_i, V_i; \theta\right) = softmax\left(\frac{Q_j K_i}{\sqrt{d_k}}\right)V_i \qquad (1)$$

where d_k is the dimension of the Key vectors, and the SoftMax function ensures that the attention weights are normalized. The cross-attention output will contain the similarity latency between omics modality i and j, and finally assembles as the updated similarity latency across the modalities with a linear layer $f(\cdot)$, denotes as $S^{(n)} = f\left(S^{(n)}, \overline{\alpha}; \theta\right)$, where $\overline{\alpha} = \{\alpha_{ij}\}_{i \neq j}$. The goal of this process is to only provide shared information across different omics modalities by distilling the unique pattern from it throughout the model updates. To do so, the shared similarity latency will also enter the multi-head self-attention modules to extract the unique information.

2.3 Preserving the Uniqueness

Each omics modality has a distinguished multi-head self-attention module to extract the unique patterns. Similar to the cross-attention score calculation, the multi-head self-attention score α_i is computed as follows:

$$\alpha_i\left(S^{(n)}, X_i; \theta\right) = Attention(Q_i, K_i, V_i; \theta) = softmax\left(\frac{Q_i K_i}{\sqrt{d_k}}\right)V_i \qquad (2)$$

Then the multi-head self-attention output will pass to the Pearson correlation test $corr(\alpha_1, \alpha_2, \ldots, \alpha_k)$ and produce an $k \times k$ correlation matrix result U. To ensure we split the unique information from the mixture $S^{(n)}$, we force the correlation matrix of multi-head self-attention score output to be orthogonal to each other. And this information will be distilled from multiple iteration steps.

3   Results

The data used in this paper is from The Cancer Genome Atlas Lung Adenocarcinoma (TCGA-LUAD) project. The sample sizes for the three omics modalities are as follows: 492 samples for DNA methylation, 576 samples for exon expression RNA-Seq, and 365 samples for protein expression (RPPA). Among these, 318 samples have data available for all three omics modalities, while 592 distinct samples have at least one omics modality available. The feature dimensions for the DNA methylation, RNA-Seq, and RPPA data are 485,577, 239,322, and 276, respectively. The data was split into training and test sets with a ratio of 4:1 one-time randomly. For the training, we set the number of epochs to 100, the batch size to 64, the number of attention heads for both self-attention and cross-attention modules to 2, and the embedding dimensions to 512.

Our results show a great performance increase in the ablation test. In an examination of predictive accuracy across various omics data modalities, Fig. 3 illustrates the C-index values derived from different combinations of data, showcasing the impact of integrating multiple data types on the predictive model's performance. This figure provides a systematic visual comparison between single, dual, and tri-modality combinations across training and testing datasets.

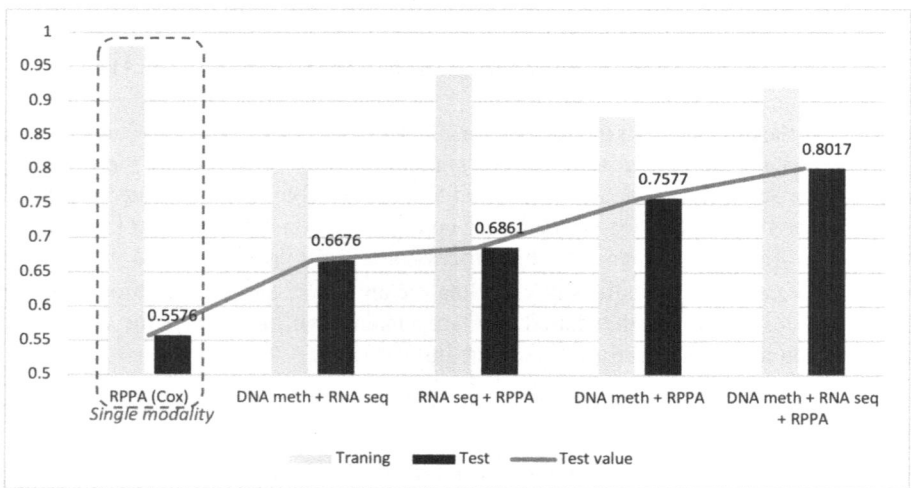

Fig. 3. Comparative C-index values for predictive models using single and multiple omics modalities. The bar charts show the performance increase in the ablation test. Training and test set with a ratio of 4:1 in the experiment.

The integration of all three omics modalities—DNA methylation, RNA sequencing (HiC), and RPPA—reaches the peak of predictive performance. The model achieves a C-index of 0.9202 in training, which further increases to 0.8017 in testing. This superior performance in the test set highlights the model's exceptional capability to generalize well beyond the training data, suggesting that a holistic multi-omics approach effectively captures the complex interactions that are pivotal for accurate survival prediction. The incremental benefits of integrating multiple omics data types into the predictive model are evident from the results depicted in Fig. 3. Each additional modality contributes to a more nuanced and comprehensive model, significantly enhancing both the accuracy and the reliability of the predictions. This suggests that multi-omics models, especially those incorporating tri-modality data, are not only viable but also potentially superior for developing robust prognostic models in biomedical research.

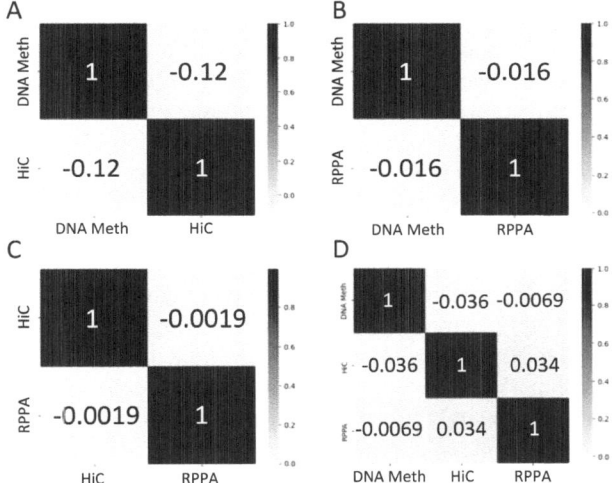

Fig. 4. Correlation heatmaps. The ablation study examined the interdependencies among different omics data types, DNA Methylation, exon expression RNA Seq (HiC), and protein expression (RPPA), in the attention-fusion multi-omics model. A) Correlation heatmap of the extracted unique information latency from DNA Methylation and HiC; B) Correlation heatmap of the extracted unique information latency from DNA Methylation and RPPA; C) Correlation heatmap of the extracted unique information latency from HiC and RPPA; D) Correlation heatmap of the extracted unique information latency from all three omics modalities.

The results presented in the heatmap matrices are from an ablation test that assesses the interactions among various omics data modalities—specifically DNA Methylation, Hi-C, and RPPA—within a multi-omics predictive model (Fig. 4). These matrices are crucial for understanding how each data type influences the model's predictive capabilities and whether there exists significant interdependency among them. In the comprehensive analysis involving all three modalities (Fig. 4D), the correlations remain notably low. The most significant negative correlation is between Hi-C and DNA Methylation

(-0.036), while the interactions between RPPA and the other two modalities show positive but very low correlations (0.034 with Hi-C and 0.00069 with DNA Methylation). These values suggest that AMMO excels in separating multi-omics information into two streams: unique and similar ones. This capability is particularly useful for exploring hidden biological connections across different omics modalities and the intricate relationships in the cellular environment.

4 Discussion

To validate the effectiveness of our proposed method, we conducted a comparative study using the TCGA-LUAD dataset. The performance of our model was measured using the concordance index (C-index), a robust metric commonly used in survival analysis to evaluate the accuracy of prognosis predictions. Our model demonstrates a superior C-index of 0.8017, outperforming all referenced studies in Table 1. For instance, Song et al. [19] report a range of C-indices from 0.619 to 0.723 using traditional Cox regression models. Our model outperforms the highest of these scores, suggesting that the integration of an attention mechanism better captures complex interdependencies and latent patterns within the multi-omics data, which linear models like Cox regression may not fully exploit. Li et al. [20] and Zhang et al. [21] both employ a combination of LASSO and Cox methods, achieving C-indices up to 0.695 and 0.796, respectively. Although Zhang et al. [21]. Present a competitive score, our model surpasses this benchmark by addressing data completeness through an innovative approach that preserves the integrity of the omics datasets. This methodological distinction highlights our model's ability to provide more robust and accurate predictions by focusing on inherent data properties and interactions, rather than filling in missing data which could introduce biases.

Among the benchmark comparisons, all the methods used the TCGA-LUAD dataset. Wen et al. [22], utilizing a straightforward Cox model, report a substantially lower C-index of 0.631. This outcome underscores the challenges traditional models face when dealing with high-dimensional and heterogeneous datasets, emphasizing the efficacy of our model in navigating these complexities through a specialized attention-based framework. Peng et al. [23] and Rączkowska et al. [24] explore deep learning methodologies, with C-indices of 0.74 and 0.723, respectively. While these approaches leverage modern computational techniques, our model achieves superior results by specifically addressing the missing modalities through a domain-aware mechanism.

However, we are aware of the disadvantages of this approach. Using orthogonal attention to extract unique information may harm performance. In our future work, we will incorporate a contrastive loss function to control extraction, ensuring that while unique representations are learned, the overall coherence and performance of the attention module are maintained. Additionally, we will apply our method to a broader range of cancer types to test the generalizability and robustness of our proposed method.

Table 1. Comparative analysis of C-index scores between our proposed model against established methods

Study	Year	Method	Reported best C-Indices on OS
Song et al., [19]	2019	Cox	0.723
Li et al., [20]	2019	LASSO + Cox	0.695
Zhang et al., [21]	2020	LASSO + Cox	**0.796**
Wen et al., [22]	2022	Cox	0.631
Peng et al., [23]	2023	Deep learning survival	0.740
Rączkowska et al., [24]	2022	DL + CNN plus H&E slides	0.723
Our study	2024	An attention-based model	**<u>0.802</u>**

References

1. Miao, Z., Humphreys, B.D., McMahon, A.P., Kim, J.: Multi-omics integration in the age of million single-cell data. Nat. Rev. Nephrol. **17**, 710–724 (2021)
2. Efremova, M., Teichmann, S.A.: Computational methods for single-cell omics across modalities. Nat. Methods **17**, 14–17 (2020)
3. Baysoy, A., Bai, Z., Satija, R., Fan, R.: The technological landscape and applications of single-cell multi-omics. Nat. Rev. Mol. Cell Biol. **24**, 695–713 (2023)
4. Park, Y.H., et al.: Longitudinal multi-omics study of palbociclib resistance in HR-positive/HER2-negative metastatic breast cancer. Genome Med. **15**, 55 (2023)
5. Dar, M.A., et al.: Multiomics technologies: role in disease biomarker discoveries and therapeutics. Brief. Funct. Genomics **22**, 76–96 (2023)
6. Badia-I-Mompel, P., et al.: Gene regulatory network inference in the era of single-cell multi-omics. Nat. Rev. Genet. **24**, 739–754 (2023)
7. Haas, R., Zelezniak, A., Iacovacci, J., Kamrad, S., Townsend, S., Ralser, M.: Designing and interpreting 'multi-omic' experiments that may change our understanding of biology. Curr. Opin. Syst. Biol. **6**, 37–45 (2017)
8. Tong, L., Wu, H., Wang, M.D.: Integrating multi-omics data by learning modality invariant representations for improved prediction of overall survival of cancer. Methods **189**, 74–85 (2021)
9. Kiessling, P., Kuppe, C.: Spatial multi-omics: novel tools to study the complexity of cardiovascular diseases. Genome Med. **16**, 14 (2024)
10. Sussulini, A., Xia, J., Orešič, M.: Editorial: Multi-omics: trends and applications in clinical research. Front. Mol. Biosci. **9**, 994239 (2022)
11. Hasin, Y., Seldin, M., Lusis, A.: Multi-omics approaches to disease. Genome Biol. **18**, (2017). https://doi.org/10.1186/s13059-017-1215-1
12. de Anda-Jáuregui, G., Hernández-Lemus, E.: Computational oncology in the multi-omics era: State of the art. Front. Oncol. **10**, 423 (2020)
13. Leonavicius, K., Nainys, J., Kuciauskas, D., Mazutis, L.: Multi-omics at single-cell resolution: comparison of experimental and data fusion approaches. Curr. Opin. Biotechnol. **55**, 159–166 (2019)
14. Leng, D., et al.: A benchmark study of deep learning-based multi-omics data fusion methods for cancer. Genome Biol. **23**, 171 (2022)

15. Carrillo-Perez, F., Morales, J.C., Castillo-Secilla, D., Gevaert, O., Rojas, I., Herrera, L.J.: Machine-learning-based late fusion on multi-omics and multi-scale data for non-small-cell lung cancer diagnosis. J. Pers. Med. **12**, 601 (2022)
16. Lin, X., Tian, T., Wei, Z., Hakonarson, H.: Clustering of single-cell multi-omics data with a multimodal deep learning method. Nat. Commun. **13**, 7705 (2022)
17. Tao, S., Rojo de la Vega, M., Chapman, E., Ooi, A., Zhang, D.D.: The effects of NRF2 modulation on the initiation and progression of chemically and genetically induced lung cancer. Mol. Carcinog. **57**, 182–192 (2018)
18. Lu, M., Zhan, X.: The crucial role of multiomic approach in cancer research and clinically relevant outcomes. EPMA J. **9**, 77–102 (2018)
19. Song, Q., et al.: Identification of an immune signature predicting prognosis risk of patients in lung adenocarcinoma. J. Transl. Med. **17**, 70 (2019)
20. Li, Y., Ge, D., Gu, J., Xu, F., Zhu, Q., Lu, C.: A large cohort study identifying a novel prognosis prediction model for lung adenocarcinoma through machine learning strategies. BMC Cancer **19**, 886 (2019)
21. Zhang, Y., et al.: Multi-omics data analyses construct TME and identify the immune-related prognosis signatures in human LUAD. Mol. Ther. Nucleic Acids. **21**, 860–873 (2020)
22. Wen, S., et al.: Four differentially expressed genes can predict prognosis and microenvironment immune infiltration in lung cancer: a study based on data from the GEO. BMC Cancer. **22**, (2022). https://doi.org/10.1186/s12885-022-09296-8
23. Peng, J., Xiao, L., Zhu, H., Han, L., Ma, H.: Determining the prognosis of Lung cancer from mutated genes using a deep learning survival model: a large multi-center study. Cancer Cell Int. **23**, 262 (2023)
24. Rączkowska, A., et al.: Deep learning-based tumor microenvironment segmentation is predictive of tumor mutations and patient survival in non-small-cell lung cancer. BMC Cancer **22**, 1001 (2022)

PD-L1 Expression Prediction Using Scalable Multi Instance Transformer

Eman Showkatian[1], Amgad Muneer[1], Maliazurina B. Saad[1], Lingzhi Hong[1,2], John V. Heymach[2], Jianjun Zhang[2], and Jia Wu[1,2(✉)]

[1] Department of Imaging Physics, MD Anderson Cancer Center, Houston, TX, USA
{jwu11,jwu11}@mdanderson.org
[2] Department of Thoracic/Head and Neck Medical Oncology, MD Anderson Cancer Center, Houston, TX, USA

Abstract. Immune checkpoint inhibitors (ICIs) have revolutionized the treatment of non-small cell lung cancer (NSCLC), benefiting 20–30% of patients. The current clinical standard for initiating ICI therapy is the assessment of Programmed Death-Ligand 1 (PD-L1) status via immunohistochemistry (IHC) on biopsy specimens. However, this invasive procedure presents risks and limitations, highlighting the need for a non-invasive alternative. This study retrospectively analyzed a cohort of 746 patients with stage IV metastatic NSCLC undergoing immunotherapy, divided into training (n = 298), internal validation (n = 75), and testing (n = 360) groups. Thirteen cases with poor image quality were excluded from the analysis. We proposed a Scalable Multi Instance Transformer (SMIT), a deep learning model, to predict PD-L1 expression from chest computed tomography (CT) scans, thereby reducing the need for invasive biopsy procedures. Compared to prior studies, our approach integrates multi-scale features from CT images, enhancing prediction accuracy and robustness. SMIT achieved superior performance in predicting PD-L1 status with precision (0.82), sensitivity (0.83), F1 score (0.83), area under the curve (AUC; 81%), and Precision-Recall AUC (0.80). SMIT's predictions for PD-L1 status ($\geq$50% or < 50%) were comparable to those derived from IHC-based PD-L1 status, validating its potential as a non-invasive diagnostic tool. Additionally, SMIT's predictions for progression-free survival (PFS) were on par with IHC-based predictions. The SMIT model represents a significant advancement in the non-invasive prediction of PD-L1 expression in NSCLC, offering a viable alternative to traditional biopsy methods. This innovation could streamline immunotherapy selection, making treatments more accessible and personalized.

Keywords: Non-Small Cell Lung Cancer · Biomarkers · Immune Checkpoint Inhibitors · Checkpoint blockade · Immunotherapy · PD-L1 expression · Scalable multi-instance transformer · Survival analysis

1 Introduction

Metastatic non-small-cell lung cancer (NSCLC) remains one of the leading causes of cancer-related mortality worldwide [1–5]. Despite advancements in targeted therapies and immunotherapies, the prognosis for patients with advanced NSCLC is often poor,

---

E. Showkatian and A. Muneer—Contributed equally

© The Author(s), under exclusive license to Springer Nature Switzerland AG 2025
J. Wu et al. (Eds.): CMMCA 2024, LNCS 15181, pp. 61–69, 2025.
https://doi.org/10.1007/978-3-031-73360-4_7

primarily due to late-stage diagnosis and the heterogeneous nature of the disease [6, 7]. One of the promising avenues in the management of NSCLC is immunotherapy, particularly treatments that target the programmed death-ligand 1 (PD-L1) pathway [8, 9, 17]. PD-L1 expression on tumor cells can inhibit the immune response, allowing cancer cells to evade immune detection [10]. As such, PD-L1 expression has become a critical biomarker for selecting patients who are most likely to benefit from immunotherapy [11, 12, 18].

Currently, the standard method for assessing PD-L1 expression involves invasive tissue biopsies, which pose several challenges, including procedural risks, sampling errors, and the inability to capture tumor heterogeneity effectively [11–13]. Given these limitations, there is an urgent need for non-invasive, reliable, and comprehensive methods to predict PD-L1 expression.

Therefore, our study aims to leverage advancements in deep learning to predict PD-L1 expression from computed tomography (CT) scans. By developing a robust deep learning model, we seek to provide a non-invasive tool that can assist clinicians in identifying patients with metastatic NSCLC who are likely to respond to PD-L1-targeted immunotherapy. This approach has the potential to transform clinical practice by improving patient selection for immunotherapy, thereby enhancing treatment outcomes, and minimizing unnecessary exposure to ineffective treatments.

Recent studies have demonstrated the feasibility of using radiomics and deep learning techniques to extract valuable prognostic and predictive information from medical imaging [14, 15]. These approaches capitalize on the ability of artificial intelligence to identify complex patterns in imaging data that are imperceptible to the human eye [20]. However, the application of deep learning specifically for predicting PD-L1 expression in NSCLC from CT scans is still in its nascent stages. Our research aims to build upon these foundational studies by developing a more accurate and clinically applicable model for predicting PD-L1 status in non-invasive way. The anticipated impact of this research is significant, offering a pathway towards more personalized and effective treatment strategies for patients with advanced lung cancer.

2   Methods

Figure 1 illustrates the overall study workflow. The methodology involves several key steps: (1) axial view extraction from the CT scan images, (2) extraction of local and global information using 2.5D multi-instance learning, (3) feature extraction leveraging the vision transformer (ViT) architecture, (4) attention aggregation to focus on relevant features, and (5) prediction of high or low PD-L1 expression levels. This comprehensive approach utilizes both local and global imaging features to enhance the accuracy and robustness of the PD-L1 prediction model. We employed 2.5D approach to capture the complex patterns associated with tumoral characteristics. It focuses on the largest tumor slice, around which a centered window is created. A sequence of 64 patches from this window is processed through the 2D network on a slice-by-slice basis. These extracted features are subsequently aggregated via an attention module before being fed into to a dense layer for classification purposes.

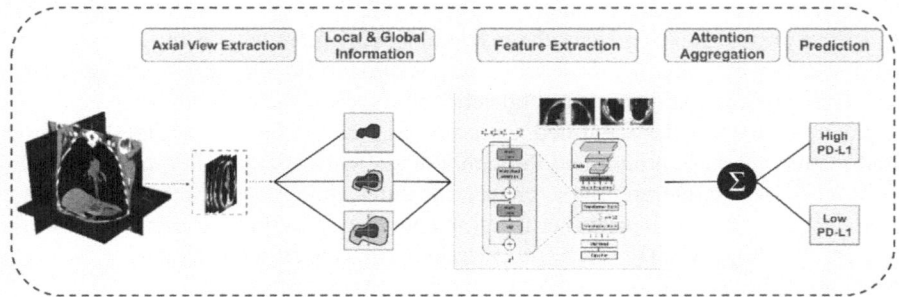

Fig. 1. Workflow of the scalable multi-instance transformer model for predicting PD-L1 expression from CT scans.

2.1 Multi Instance Learning Formulation

Problem formulation: Typically, in binary supervised learning, the goal is to create a model capable of predicting the binary target variable, y (which can be either 0 or 1), for any given input instance, $\mathbf{x} \in \mathbb{R}^D$, within a D-dimensional space. In contrast, MIL deals with a collection of instances known as a bag, represented as $X = \{X_1,..., X_K\}$, where the instances within the bag are independent and unordered [19]. The size of the bag, denoted by K, may differ across bags. Each bag is assigned a single binary label, Y. Although individual labels $(y_1,..., y_K)$ are presumed to exist for each instance within a bag, with y_k belonging to $\{0, 1\}$ for $k = 1, ..., K$, they are not accessible during the training phase and thus remain unknown. The fundamental assumption of MIL in our study can be expressed as follows:

$$Y = \begin{cases} 0, \text{ iff } \sum_k y_k = 0 \\ 1, \quad \text{otherwise} \end{cases} \tag{1}$$

These assumptions indicate that a MIL model must be permutation-invariant. Additionally, the two statements can be succinctly rephrased using the maximum operator:

$$Y = \max_k \{y_k\} \tag{2}$$

Learning a model that optimizes an objective based on the maximum over instance labels poses at least two challenges. First, all gradient-based learning methods would struggle with vanishing gradients. Second, this approach is only appropriate when an instance-level classifier is employed. To simplify the learning problem, we propose training a MIL model by optimizing the log-likelihood function. Here, the bag label is modeled using the Bernoulli distribution with parameter $\theta(X) \in [0, 1]$, representing the probability of $Y = 1$ given the bag of instances X.

After extraction, features are articulated in a matrix, with each row encapsulating the feature descriptors for an individual image instance. The matrix embodies a comprehensive feature space with dimensions reflective of tumor masks, boundaries, and contextual information; all critical determinants in assessing PD-L1 expression. An attention module is then invoked to aggregate these features. This module selectively weights the feature vectors, emphasizing those with the most prognostic relevance to PD-L1 expression. The output is a singular, consolidated feature vector that embodies the essence of the salient characteristics identified across the aggregated instances (Fig. 2). The distilled feature vector is propagated through a neural network classifier, a multi-layered construct poised to interpret the aggregated features and render a binary prediction of PD-L1 expression. The binary classification demarcates the PD-L1 expression level as high (PD-L $\geq$ 50) or low (PD-L1 < 50), thresholds that are critically aligned with clinical decision-making paradigms in lung cancer treatment pathways.

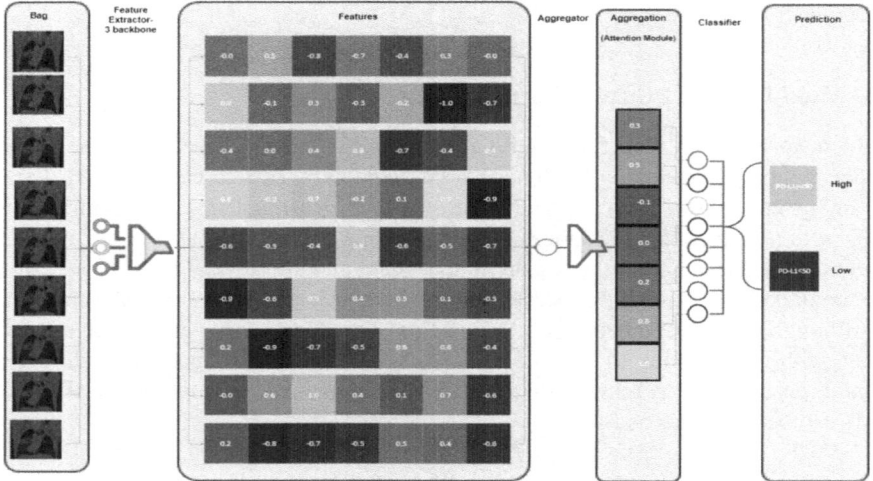

Fig. 2. Multiple instances learning pipeline.

2.2   Patient Cohorts and Study Design

This retrospective modeling study utilized comprehensive clinicopathological data, radiographic reports, and prognostic information sourced from the Epic electronic medical record system. Baseline CT images, collected from the IntelliSpace PACS by Philips, served as the foundational dataset for model development and validation. Patients with metastatic NSCLC who were treated with ICI alone or in combination with chemotherapy were identified from the MD Anderson GEMINI database, which includes extensive clinicopathological, radiological, and survival information, with patients enrolled between January 1, 2014, and February 29, 2020.

A total of 746 NSCLC patient's cohort were utilized (Stage-IV), cases with poor image quality (n = 13) were excluded from the analysis. The remaining patients (n = 733) were divided into training (n = 298), internal validation (n = 75), and testing (n =

360). The PD-L1 expression levels were also defined as high (PD-L1 $= 50$) or low (PD-L1 < 50), thresholds that are critically aligned with clinical decision-making standards in lung cancer treatment pathways [16].

3   Experiments and Results

In our study, we developed an AI model, SMIT, designed to serve as a non-invasive surrogate for IHC-derived PD-L1 status, thereby eliminating the need for invasive tissue sampling. This innovative approach allows patients to ascertain their PD-L1 status without undergoing surgical procedures. When benchmarked against the ground truth derived from immunohistochemistry (IHC), the prognostic power of our AI model demonstrated capabilities that were roughly comparable to those of the traditional invasive methods. Therefore, SMIT proves particularly valuable in scenarios involving tissue scarcity or in cases where patients opt out of surgical interventions. Three models were benchmarked in predicting PD-L1 expression (Fig. 3): a clinical model, a classical radiomics model, and the proposed SMIT model. The CT-derived SMIT signature outperforms both the radiomics and clinical model by a large margin.

The clinical model, which shows lower performance across most metrics, particularly in Precision (0.19) and F1 Score (0.29); the radiomics model, which exhibits moderate performance improvements, with the highest metric being AUC (0.73); and the SMIT model, which demonstrates superior performance across all metrics, especially in sensitivity (0.83) and precision-recall AUC (0.80) (Fig. 3). The SMIT Combined approach, which integrates all feature extraction methods and achieves consistently high performance across all metrics, particularly in AUC (0.83) and precision-recall AUC (0.80).

Additionally, Fig. 4 (a) shows the ROC curves comparing the clinical model (AUC $= 0.48$), radiomics model (AUC $= 0.57$), and SMIT model (AUC $= 0.81$), with the SMIT model demonstrating superior performance. Figure 4 (b) presents ROC curves for different attention mechanisms in the SMIT model: tumor boundary (AUC $= 0.79$), local attention (AUC $= 0.79$), global attention (AUC $= 0.78$), and the combined SMIT model (AUC $= 0.81$), showing that the combined model performs the best.

Figure 5 illustrates the robustness of the SMIT model in predicting PD-L1 status, the confusion matrices in Fig. 5(a) through 5(f) compare the predictive capabilities of different models. The clinical model (Fig. 5a) and the radiomics model (Fig. 5b) have higher misclassification rates. In contrast, Fig. 5(c), 5(d), and 5(e) show components of the SMIT model—tumor boundary, local attention, and global attention—with higher accuracy and fewer misclassifications. Figure 5(f) presents the combined SMIT model, integrating all attention mechanisms, achieving the highest overall performance and minimal misclassifications. This comparison underscores the superior predictive capabilities of the SMIT model in accurately predicting PD-L1 expression.

Figure 6 illustrates the PFS survival curves stratified by PD-L1 expression levels. In the training cohort (Fig. 6a), patients with high PD-L1 expression (PD-High) exhibit significantly better PFS outcomes compared to those with low PD-L1 expression (PD-Low), as indicated by a p-value of less than 0.001. The SMIT model's predictions closely mirror this distinction, with a p-value of 0.002, underscoring its strong prognostic power. The testing cohort set (Fig. 6b) confirms the model's robustness, showing

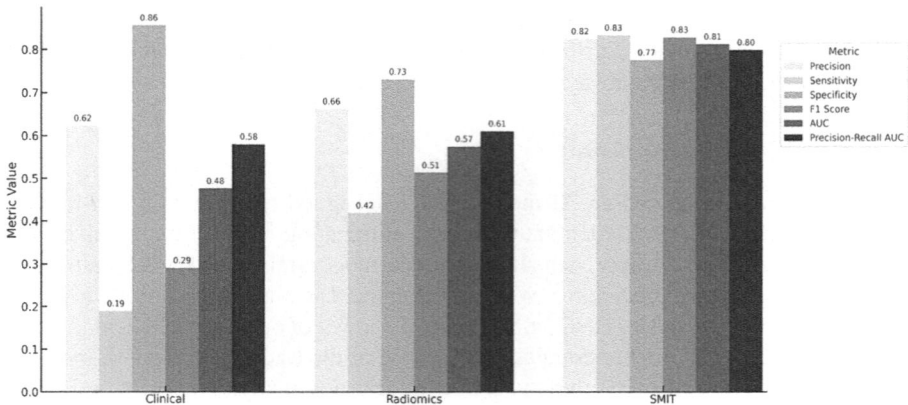

Fig. 3. Performance comparison of models in PD-L1 Expression: Comparison of Clinical, Radiomics, and SMIT models across various performance metrics. The SMIT model outperforms both clinical and radiomics models in all metrics.

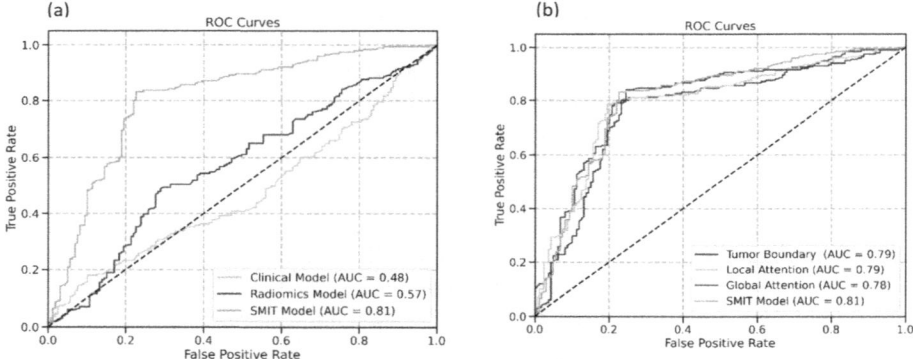

Fig. 4. Performance Comparison Using ROC and Precision-Recall Curves. (a) ROC curves for Clinical, Radiomics, and SMIT models. (b) ROC curves for various attention mechanisms within the SMIT model.

similar significant differences in survival outcomes, with the SMIT model yielding a p-value of 0.006. In the overall validation set (Fig. 6c), the model maintains its predictive accuracy, with PFS curves showing significant differences between PD-High and PD-Low patients (p-value < 0.001), demonstrating its ability to generalize to independent cohorts. Overall, the SMIT model reliably stratifies patients by PD-L1 status, highlighting its potential for broad clinical application in guiding immunotherapy decisions. The strong alignment between the model's predictions and the ground truth data, reflected in consistently significant p-values, validates the model's reliability and robustness. This non-invasive predictive tool not only enhances treatment personalization but also holds the potential to improve overall patient outcomes by optimizing the selection process for immunotherapy.

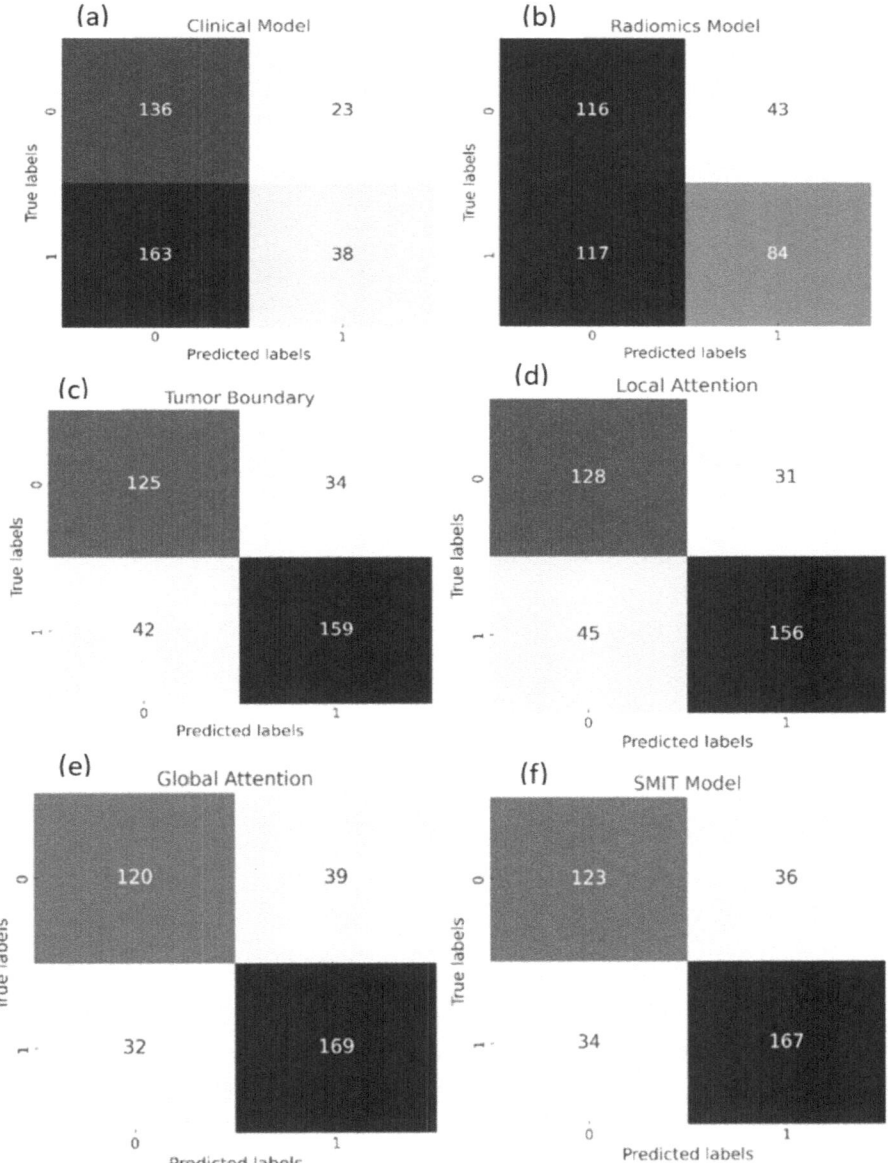

Fig. 5. (a-f) Confusion matrices illustrating the predictive capabilities of different models: (a) Clinical Model, (b) Radiomics Model, (c) Tumor Boundary, (d) Local Attention, (e) Global Attention, and (f) SMIT Model, with the SMIT model showing the highest overall performance.

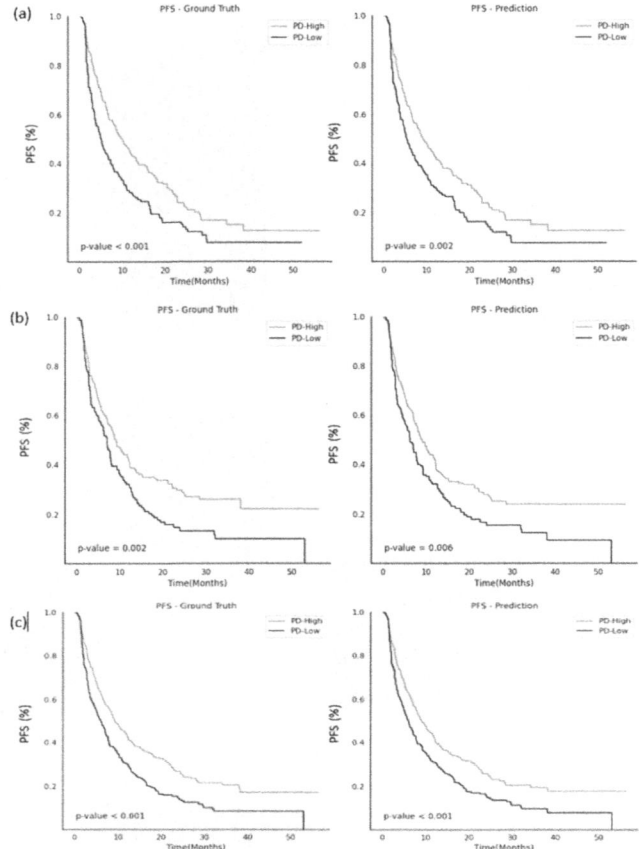

Fig. 6. PFS survival analysis stratified by PD-L1 expression levels. (a) Training cohort; (b) Testing cohort: (c) Overall validation set.

4 Conclusion

This study highlights the transformative potential of the SMIT model in predicting PD-L1 expression from chest CT scans in metastatic NSCLC patients. Utilizing advanced deep learning techniques and integrating multi-scale features, the SMIT model achieves unprecedented accuracy and robustness, outperforming traditional clinical and radiomics models. Our evaluation on large population confirms its adaptability and reliability, solidifying its role as a non-invasive diagnostic tool. Accurately predicting PD-L1 expression non-invasively can streamline immunotherapy selection, ensuring patients receive the most appropriate treatments while minimizing the risks of invasive biopsies. The SMIT model's superior performance in predicting PFS further validates its clinical utility, offering a pathway to more precise and personalized therapeutic strategies. Future work will focus on refining the model and exploring its application in other cancer types.

References

1. Bar, J., et al.: Long-term survival of patients with metastatic non-small-cell lung cancer over five decades. J. Oncol. **2021**(1), 7836264 (2021)
2. Arbour, K.C., Riely, G.J.: Systemic therapy for locally advanced and metastatic non–small cell lung cancer: a review. JAMA **322**(8), 764–774 (2019)
3. Planchard, D., et al.: Metastatic non-small cell lung cancer: ESMO clinical practice guidelines for diagnosis, treatment and follow-up. Ann. Oncol. **29**, iv192-iv237 (2018)
4. Gridelli, C., et al.: Non-small-cell lung cancer. Nat. Rev. Dis. Primers. **1**(1), 1–16 (2015)
5. Chaft, J.E., Rimner, A., Weder, W., Azzoli, C.G., Kris, M.G., Cascone, T.: Evolution of systemic therapy for stages I-III non-metastatic non-small-cell lung cancer. Nat. Rev. Clin. Oncol. **18**(9), 547–557 (2021)
6. Megyesfalvi, Z., et al.: Clinical insights into small cell lung cancer: Tumor heterogeneity, diagnosis, therapy, and future directions. CA a cancer j. Clin. **73**(6), 620–652 (2023)
7. Russano, M., et al.: Immunotherapy for metastatic non-small cell lung cancer: therapeutic advances and biomarkers. Curr. Oncol. **30**(2), 2366–2387 (2023)
8. Shen, X., Zhang, L., Li, J., Li, Y., Wang, Y., Xu, Z.X.: Recent findings in the regulation of programmed death ligand 1 expression. Front. Immunol. **10**, 1337 (2019)
9. Wang, T., et al.: Development of inhibitors of the programmed cell death-1/programmed cell death-ligand 1 signaling pathway. J. Med. Chem. **62**(4), 1715–1730 (2018)
10. Chen, S., et al.: Mechanisms regulating PD-L1 expression on tumor and immune cells. J. Immunother. Cancer **7**, 1–12 (2019)
11. Meng, X., Huang, Z., Teng, F., Xing, L., Yu, J.: Predictive biomarkers in PD-1/PD-L1 checkpoint blockade immunotherapy. Cancer Treat. Rev. **41**(10), 868–876 (2015)
12. Doroshow, D.B., et al.: PD-L1 as a biomarker of response to immune-checkpoint inhibitors. Nat. Rev. Clin. Oncol. **18**(6), 345–362 (2021)
13. Zhao, L., et al.: Concordance of PD-L1 status between image-guided percutaneous biopsies and matched surgical specimen in non-small cell lung cancer. Front. Oncol. **10**, 551367 (2021)
14. Afshar, P., Mohammadi, A., Plataniotis, K.N., Oikonomou, A., Benali, H.: From handcrafted to deep-learning-based cancer radiomics: challenges and opportunities. IEEE Signal Process. Mag. **36**(4), 132–160 (2019)
15. Saad, M.B., et al.: Predicting benefit from immune checkpoint inhibitors in patients with non-small-cell lung cancer by CT-based ensemble deep learning: a retrospective study. Lancet Digital Health **5**(7), e404–e420 (2023)
16. Lantuejoul, S., et al.: PD-L1 testing for lung cancer in 2019: perspective from the IASLC pathology committee. J. Thorac. Oncol. **15**(4), 499–519 (2020)
17. Wu, J., Mayer, A. T., Li, R.: Integrated imaging and molecular analysis to decipher tumor microenvironment in the era of immunotherapy. In: Seminars in cancer biology, Vol. 84, pp. 310–328. Academic Press (September 2022)
18. Al-Tashi, Q., et al.: Machine learning models for the identification of prognostic and predictive cancer biomarkers: a systematic review. Int. J. Mol. Sci. **24**(9), 7781 (2023)
19. Waqas, M., Ahmed, S. U., Tahir, M. A., Wu, J., Qureshi, R.: Exploring Multiple Instance Learning (MIL): a brief survey. Expert Syst. Appl. **250**, 123893 (2024)
20. Chen, M.M., et al.: Artificial intelligence in oncologic imaging. Eur. J. Radiol. Open **9**, 100441 (2022)

Improving Single-Source Domain Generalization via Anatomy-Guided Texture Augmentation for Cervical Tumor Segmentation

Lixue Qin[1,2], Zhibo Xiao[3], Nazar Zaki[4,5], Yaoqin Xie[1], and Wenjian Qin[1(✉)]

[1] Shenzhen Institute of Advanced Technology, Chinese Academy of Sciences, Shenzhen, China
lx.qin@siat.ac.cn
[2] University of Chinese Academy of Sciences, Beijing, China
{yq.xie,wj.qin}@siat.ac.cn
[3] Department of Radiology, The First Affiliated Hospital of Chongqing Medical University, Chongqing 400016, China
202530@cqmu.edu.cn
[4] Department of Computer Science and Software Engineering, College of Information Technology, United Arab Emirates University, Al Ain 15551, UAE
nzaki@uaeu.ac.ae
[5] Aspire Precision Medicine Research Institute Abu Dhabi, Abu Dhabi, UAE

Abstract. Single-Source domain generalization in medical image segmentation has been studied as a more practical configuration to solve domain shift issues in clinical applications. Data augmentation plays an important role in improving the diversity of training data. Recent data augmentation methods aim to randomize or disrupt the texture of images to encourage models to focus more on shape features, which are considered domain-invariant. It's worth noting that texture features such as intensity variations are crucial cues for distinguishing the boundaries between the tumor and normal tissues. However, these features are often disrupted or compromised in existing methods. To effectively leverage these texture features and enhance the performance of the model, we propose a novel anatomy-guided texture augmentation (AGTA) method. Specifically, as imaging parameters vary, different organs or tissues may exhibit varying changes in intensity, while the intensity variations within each organ or tissue tend to remain consistent. To simulate this, we partition different organs into distinct regions based on the anatomical information of the image. Each region is then assigned random variations. We evaluated our method against other SDG methods in cross-modality and cross-center cervical tumor segmentation experiments. Our results show that our method outperforms all competing methods by a large margin.

Keywords: Single-Source Domain Generalization · Data Augmentation · Cervical Tumor Segmentation · Medical Image Segmentation · Anatomy-guided Texture Augmentation

© The Author(s), under exclusive license to Springer Nature Switzerland AG 2025
J. Wu et al. (Eds.): CMMCA 2024, LNCS 15181, pp. 70–79, 2025.
https://doi.org/10.1007/978-3-031-73360-4_8

1   Introduction

Cervical cancer is a significant public health concern, ranking as the second leading cause of cancer death among women aged 20–39 years, and the fourth leading cause of cancer death for women aged 40–49 years [19]. In 2022, estimated 13,740 women in the United States were diagnosed with cervical cancer, resulting in approximately 4300 related deaths [23]. Meanwhile, in China, around 111,820 women were diagnosed with cervical cancer, and over 61,500 died from the disease that same year [23]. Magnetic resonance imaging (MRI) plays an important role in the diagnosis and treatment of cervical cancer [18]. Continuous collection of imaging data from the patient is required to accurately determine the location, size, and changes of the tumor throughout the whole process of the treatment. To improve the consistency of segmentation results and save costs, automatic segmentation has become crucial, and in recent years, deep learning-based medical image segmentation models have been developed and advanced [7,9,13].

Existing deep learning-based models are based on the i.i.d. assumption [10], which assumes that the training and testing data are independently and identically distributed. Medical images often exhibit domain gaps due to factors such as scan parameters, instrument types, and imaging modalities. Therefore, when deploying a trained model directly to an unseen new domain, there is a significant degradation in the model's performance. Various methods such as unsupervised domain adaptation (UDA) [5,11,22] and domain generalization (DG) [21,25,26] have been studied to improve the generalization of models. UDA [11,22] requires access to unlabeled or limited labeled data from the target domain during the training phase and the model needs to be retrained as the target domain shifts over time. Multi-source Domain Generalization (MDG) [6,16] uses data from multiple source domains during training to enhance the model's generalization. These requirements make it difficult to deploy UDA or MDG in clinical practice due to concerns over patient privacy and the costs associated with data collection. Therefore, in our paper, we consider a more practical and challenging approach, Single-Source Domain Generalization (SDG) [1,15,20,24,27,28].

SDG aims to train robust models from only one source domain data which can perform well in a new unseen target domain. A common approach is to perform one or several data augmentation methods on the source domain images to generate new images, in order to enrich the training data. The Dual-norm [28] method uses Bézier curves [14] to augment the images and classify them into "source-similar domain" and "source-dissimilar domain". CISDG [15] proposed a global intensity non-linear augmentation (GIN) module and an interventional pseudo-correlation augmentation (IPA) method to effectively increase the texture diversity of the images and remove spurious correlations. GIN augments images by using random-weighted shallow convolutional networks. IPA generates random pseudo-correlation maps used as pixel-wise coefficients for blending two GIN-transformed images. SLAug [20] proposes a class-level transformation strategy based on label information and an image fusion strategy based on saliency maps to guide the transformations.

The existing augmentation methods primarily aim to randomize or disrupt the texture of images, thereby encouraging the model to focus more on shape features, which are considered domain-invariant. However, instead of separating shape features and texture features, certain studies [8,29] have recognized the importance of incorporating both aspects to enhance the generation of segmentation models. In the case of cervical tumors, which are abnormal tissue growths with potentially smaller differences in morphology and density compared to surrounding normal tissues, we believe that texture features such as intensity variations can play a crucial role in distinguishing between the tumor and normal tissues.

Medical images, such as CT and MRI scans, are typically captured in grayscale. The varying tissue compositions of different organs result in inherent gray-scale differences between them in the images. Moreover, different medical imaging modalities (e.g., T1, T2) exhibit varying sensitivity to factors like water content and protein composition, leading to distinct gray-scale variations within the same organ across modalities [17]. Considering these characteristics of medical images, we try to explore a novel data augmentation strategy that can enhance the diversity of feature variations among different tissues while maintaining internal consistency within the tissues.

In this paper, We propose an anatomy-guided texture augmentation (AGTA) method for medical images. Specifically, we partition different organs into distinct regions using the anatomical information of the image. Each region is then assigned random variations to generate the new augmented image. By combining our method with global transformations based on Bézier curves, we've implemented a single-source domain generalization network framework to achieve cross-modality and cross-center tasks of cervical tumor segmentation. In summary, we contribute in the following aspects:

- We propose a novel anatomy-guided texture augmentation (AGTA) method. We try to maintain part of texture information instead of only using shape information when augmenting images.
- To the best of our knowledge, We apply single-source domain generalization methods to cervical tumor segmentation.
- We combine our proposed method with a global transformation based on Bézier curves to augment the images and conduct cross-center and cross-modality experiments on cervical tumor data. The results show that our method outperforms the current state-of-the-art methods.

2   Method

2.1   Anatomy-Guided Texture Augmentation

Figure 1 illustrates the implementation of our proposed anatomy-guided texture augmentation (AGTA) method. For each image x in the source domain, we calculate the gradient map g_x of the image. The function is defined as follows:

$$g_x = \sqrt{(x * S_h)^2 + (x * S_v)^2} \tag{1}$$

where S_h denotes the horizontal Sobel operator and S_v denotes the vertical Sobel operator. We set the local maxima in the gradient map as seed points, and subsequently apply the watershed algorithm on the source image, partitioning the image into different regions. Subsequently, assign random coefficients to each region, resulting in a weighted intensity augmentation map m based on anatomical information. Random coefficients are generated within the ranges of $[-1, -0.2] \cup [0.2, 1]$, taking into account that grayscale variations can become excessively small when coefficients approach zero. Finally, we perform a Hadamard product between the original image and the weighted segmentation map to obtain the enhanced image x_a. The product can be represented as:

$$x_a = x \odot m \tag{2}$$

By utilizing the gradient map and the watershed algorithm, we can effectively differentiate various organ regions, allowing for targeted transformations in different areas.

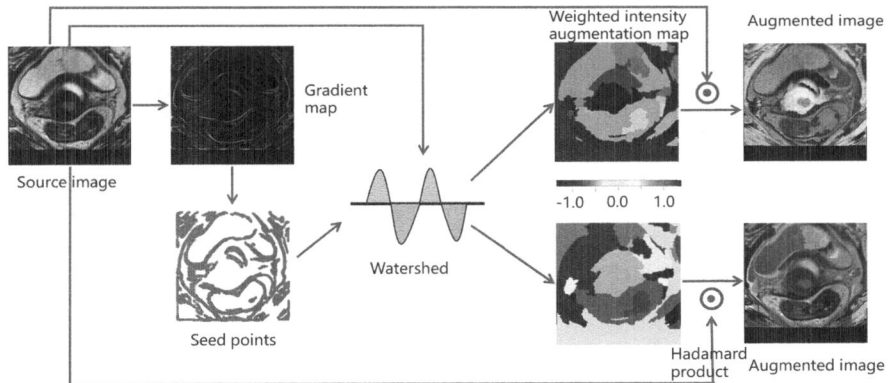

Fig. 1. Illustration of proposed boundary-based region-level augmentation. The watershed algorithm divides an image into different regions or objects based on the grayscale values and local characteristics of the image. We get a weighted intensity augmentation map by assigning random coefficients to each region.

2.2 The Overall Framework

The overall framework is shown in Fig. 2. We combine our proposed transformation and global transformation to augment images. We choose the Cubic Bézier Curve [14], a smooth and monotonic function, as our global transformation function. The Cubic Bézier Curve is a parametric curve defined by four control points: P_0, P_1, P_2, and P_3. The function is defined as follows:

$$B(t) = \sum_{i=0}^{3} \binom{3}{i} P_i (1-t)^{3-i} t^i, t \in [-1, 1] \tag{3}$$

where $B(t)$ represents the position of the curve at a given parameter value t, which ranges from -1 to 1. P_0 and P_3 are the start and end points of the curve. P_1 and P_2 are the two intermediate control points that define the shape and curvature of the Bézier curve, whose values are randomly generated from $[-1, 1]$. We set $p = 0.2$ as the probability of performing the global transformation and $p = 0.8$ as the probability of performing our proposed region-level transformation. The segmentation loss is calculated by computing the Dice loss and the cross-entropy loss on the obtained segmentation results. The segmentation loss can be written as:

$$L_{seg}(x, y) = L_{dice}(x, y) + L_{ce}(x, y) \qquad (4)$$

To ensure consistent segmentation results for the augmented images of the same original image, we also include a consistency loss. This loss is computed as the Kullback-Leibler (KL) divergence between the segmentation results of different augmented images. The function can be written as:

$$L_{consist}(x, y) = D(p(y \mid f_\theta(x^{a1})) \parallel p(y \mid f_\theta(x^{a2}))) \qquad (5)$$

where $D(\bullet \parallel \bullet)$ represents the Kullback-Leibler (KL) divergence, which measures the difference between two probability distributions. x^{a1} and x^{a2} represent the augmented images of source image x. The overall training process is as follows: In each training epoch, we get two augmented images from every original image. There is an 80% probability of using our proposed method, and a 20% probability of applying global transformation. The two augmented images and the original image are then concatenated along the channel axis to form a 3-channel image, which is input to the network for training. The total loss is the combination of the segmentation loss and the consistency loss, which can be written as follows:

$$L_{overall}(x, y) = L_{seg}(x, y) + \lambda_{consist} * L_{consist}(x, y) \qquad (6)$$

where the weighting coefficient $\lambda_{consist}$ is set to be 10.0 [15]. The segmentation loss is calculated as the average of the segmentation losses between the original image and the two corresponding augmented images. The consistency loss

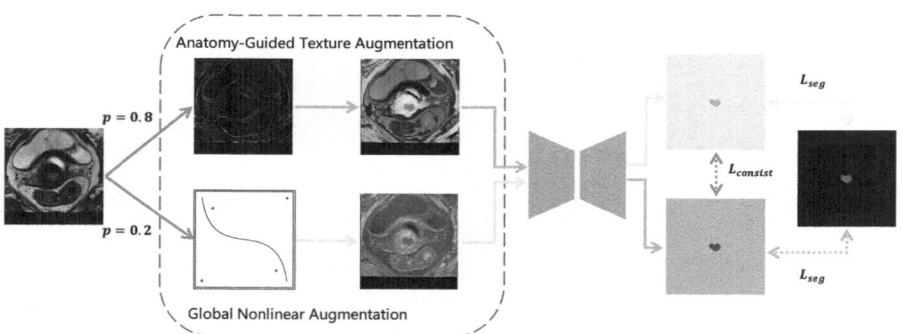

Fig. 2. Overall framework of our method. In each epoch, two augmented images are generated for each original image and the augmentation method is randomly selected.

is computed as the average of the consistency losses between each pair of the original image and two augmented images.

3 Experiments and Results

3.1 Dataset

The TCGA-CESC dataset [2, 12] and the CervicalMRI-CQ [3, 4] dataset are used for this study. The TCGA-CESC dataset comprises multiple instances of MR imaging data from a total of 54 patients diagnosed with cervical cancer. The dataset encompasses several sectional views of the patients. In our study, we select the axial view of data in T1 and T2 modalities. The dataset consists of 54 volumes in the T1 modality and 85 volumes in the T2 modality. The CervicalMRI-CQ dataset contains 100 volumes of T2 modality. The cancer types observed in the two datasets both include Cervical Squamous Cell Carcinoma and Endocervical Adenocarcinoma.

For all the original body data, we initially standardized the orientation. To address any off-resonance issues, we clipped the top 0.5% of the histograms. Subsequently, we performed resampling to achieve a unified spacing. We resized the data based on the center points of the labels and sliced them into 256×256 2D slices. To facilitate the subsequent data augmentation operations, we performed min-max normalization on the image slices to scale the values within the range of $[-1, 1]$. After preprocessing, for the TCGA-CESC dataset, we got 458 image slices in the T1 modality and 1081 image slices in the T2 modality. And 487 image slices in the T2 modality were obtained after preprocessing for the CervicalMRI-CQ dataset.

We selected the T2 modality data from the TCGA-CESC dataset as the source domain. The T1 modality data from the TCGA-CESC dataset was used as the target domain for the cross-modality segmentation experiments. The T2 modality data from the CervicalMRI-CQ dataset was used as the target domain for the cross-center segmentation experiments. The source domain data was divided into training and validation sets in a ratio of 80% and 20%. We used the entire data from the target domain to test the trained model.

All the methods evaluated (including "ERM" and "Supervised") conducted conventional augmentations including Brightness, Contrast, and Additive Gaussian Noise. Our proposed method was applied after these common augmentations.

3.2 Implementation Details

We employed U-Net with an EfficientNet-b2 backbone as our segmentation network, the same as CISDG [15] and SLAug [20]. We also configured the same optimizer and dynamic learning rate. For all experiments, we set the batch size as 20 and implemented our model with the PyTorch framework on an NVIDIA RTX A6000 GPU with 48 GB memory.

3.3   Evaluation Metrics

To achieve a comprehensive evaluation, We computed the Dice similarity coefficient (Dice), 95% Hausdorff distance (HD95), and average surface distance (ASD) between the prediction and the ground truth.

3.4   Results and Analysis

We compare our proposed method with the baseline empirical risk minimization (ERM) and the state-or-the-art methods (e.g. MixStyle [27], CISDG [15], and SLAug [20]). Table 1 displays the quantitative performance of different methods. Overall, our method outperforms the other methods in both cross-domain cervical tumor segmentation tasks. To be specific, in the cross-modality task, our method achieves an improvement of 2.1 Dice score compared with the best performing of 74.0 Dice score from CISDG. The cross-center tasks are relatively more challenging. The method CISDG, which performs well in the cross-modality task, exhibits the worst Dice score in the cross-center task. In contrast, our method maintains good stability and achieves the best results across all three evaluation metrics in the cross-center task. There is only one label available in the data and the tumor label is likely to be very small. We believe this can render the ineffectiveness of the label-based multi-scale augmentation method in SLAug.

Table 1. Comparison of different methods

Method	Cross-Modality (CESC T2 to CESC T1)			Cross-Center (CESC T2 to CQ T2)		
	Dice(%)↑	HD95(mm)↓	ASD(mm)↓	Dice(%)↑	HD95(mm)↓	ASD(mm)↓
Supervised	78.9	10.7	2.32	72.9	8.67	2.09
ERM	68.5	26.0	7.19	50.9	24.8	9.50
MixStyle(2021)	69.2	23.3	6.04	50.5	25.7	8.53
CISDG(2022)	74.0	11.9	2.62	44.9	21.7	8.75
SLAug(2023)	69.4	13.3	3.05	47.2	26.5	9.33
Ours	**76.1**	**8.82**	**1.80**	**54.0**	**17.0**	**5.14**

Figure 3 compares the visualization results of our proposed method and other methods. The figure reveals that the other methods struggle to effectively differentiate the tumor from the surrounding normal tissues. They appear insensitive to the intensity variations between these regions and tend to identify the whole organ region. We speculate that this is potentially due to the fact that such intensity differences might be disrupted in other augmentation methods, causing the model to pay less attention to them. In contrast, our method demonstrates superior capability in detecting subtle intensity differences between the tumor and the surrounding normal tissues, resulting in more accurate segmentation results compared to other methods. Consequently, our method not only improves the

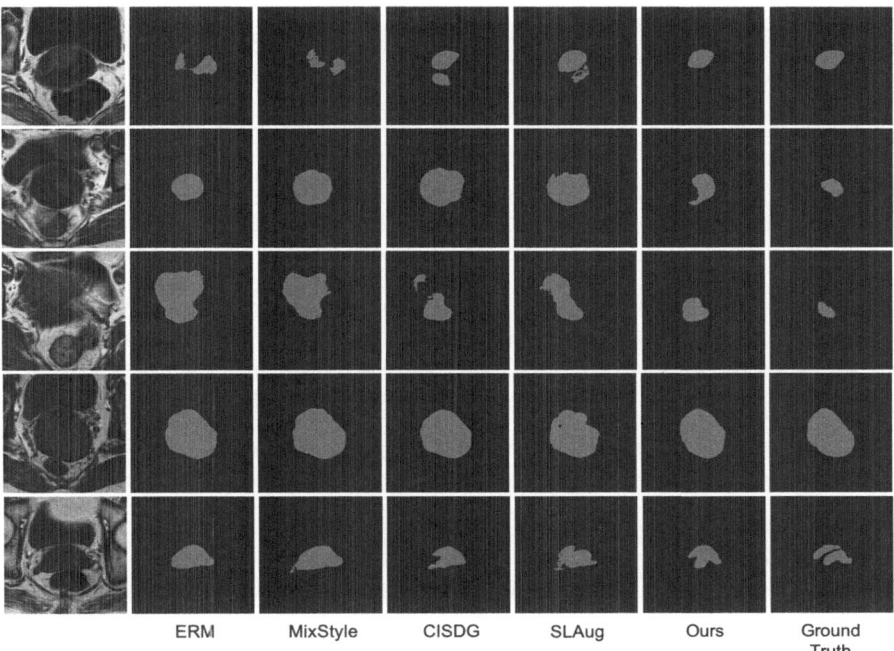

ERM   MixStyle   CISDG   SLAug   Ours   Ground
Truth

Fig. 3. Visualization of the results from different methods

Dice score but also achieves lower HD95 and ASD values, indicating enhanced spatial agreement between the predicted segmentation and the ground truth masks.

4   Conclusion

Our method relies on the anatomical information to divide the image into different regions and apply intensity transformations accordingly. By maintaining internal consistency within the tissues, our method enables the model to effectively utilize the texture features to distinguish the boundaries between the tumor and the surrounding normal tissues, in contrast to other methods. Our method outperforms the current state-of-the-art in both cross-modality and cross-center cervical cancer tumor segmentation tasks and achieves the best spatial consistency between the predicted segmentation and the ground truth.

Acknowledgments. This work was supported by the National Natural Science Foundation of China (No. U20A20373); and the Youth Innovation Promotion Association CAS (2022365), and Shenzhen-Hong Kong Joint Lab on Intelligence Computational Analysis for Tumor Imaging (E3G111); The authors express sincere gratitude for the support provided by the United Arab Emirates University (UAEU) through the joint collaboration grant number G00003558.

Disclosure of Interests. The authors have no competing interests to declare that are relevant to the content of this article.

References

1. Chen, C., Li, Z., Ouyang, C., Sinclair, M., Bai, W., Rueckert, D.: MaxStyle: adversarial style composition for robust medical image segmentation. In: Wang, L., Dou, Q., Fletcher, P.T., Speidel, S., Li, S. (eds.) MICCAI 2022. LNCS, vol. 13435, pp. 151–161. Springer, Cham (2022). https://doi.org/10.1007/978-3-031-16443-9_15
2. Clark, K., et al.: The cancer imaging archive (TCIA): maintaining and operating a public information repository. J. Digit. Imaging **26**, 1045–1057 (2013)
3. He, Z., et al.: The value of HPV genotypes combined with clinical indicators in the classification of cervical squamous cell carcinoma and adenocarcinoma. BMC Cancer **22**(1), 776 (2022)
4. He, Z., Lv, F., Li, C., Liu, Y., Xiao, Z.: The value of ensemble learning model based on conventional non-contrast MRI in the pathological grading of cervical cancer. In: Qin, W., Zaki, N., Zhang, F., Wu, J., Yang, F., Li, C. (eds.) CMMCA 2023. LNCS, vol. 14243, pp. 31–41. Springer, Cham (2023). https://doi.org/10.1007/978-3-031-45087-7_4
5. Hu, S., Liao, Z., Xia, Y.: Domain specific convolution and high frequency reconstruction based unsupervised domain adaptation for medical image segmentation. In: Wang, L., Dou, Q., Fletcher, P.T., Speidel, S., Li, S. (eds.) MICCAI 2022. LNCS, vol. 13437, pp. 650–659. Springer, Cham (2022). https://doi.org/10.1007/978-3-031-16449-1_62
6. Hu, S., Liao, Z., Zhang, J., Xia, Y.: Domain and content adaptive convolution based multi-source domain generalization for medical image segmentation. IEEE Trans. Med. Imaging **42**(1), 233–244 (2022)
7. Kano, Y., Ikushima, H., Sasaki, M., Haga, A.: Automatic contour segmentation of cervical cancer using artificial intelligence. J. Radiat. Res. **62**(5), 934–944 (2021)
8. Kim, S., Kim, D.H., Kim, H.: Texture learning domain randomization for domain generalized segmentation. In: Proceedings of the IEEE/CVF International Conference on Computer Vision, pp. 677–687 (2023)
9. Lin, Y.C., et al.: Deep learning for fully automated tumor segmentation and extraction of magnetic resonance radiomics features in cervical cancer. Eur. Radiol. **30**, 1297–1305 (2020)
10. Litjens, G., et al.: A survey on deep learning in medical image analysis. Med. Image Anal. **42**, 60–88 (2017)
11. Liu, X., et al.: Deep unsupervised domain adaptation: a review of recent advances and perspectives. APSIPA Trans. Sig. Inf. Process. **11**(1) (2022)
12. Lucchesi, F.R., Aredes, N.D.: The cancer genome atlas cervical squamous cell carcinoma and endocervical adenocarcinoma collection (TCGA-CESC) (2016). https://doi.org/10.7937/K9/TCIA.2016.SQ4M8YP4. https://www.cancerimagingarchive.net/collection/tcga-cesc/
13. Ma, C.Y., et al.: Deep learning-based auto-segmentation of clinical target volumes for radiotherapy treatment of cervical cancer. J. Appl. Clin. Med. Phys. **23**(2), e13470 (2022)
14. Mortenson, M.E.: Mathematics for Computer Graphics Applications. G - Reference, Information and Interdisciplinary Subjects Series. Industrial Press (1999). https://books.google.com.hk/books?id=YmQy799flPkC

15. Ouyang, C., et al.: Causality-inspired single-source domain generalization for medical image segmentation. IEEE Trans. Med. Imaging **42**(4), 1095–1106 (2022)
16. Seo, S., Suh, Y., Kim, D., Kim, G., Han, J., Han, B.: Learning to optimize domain specific normalization for domain generalization. In: Vedaldi, A., Bischof, H., Brox, T., Frahm, J.-M. (eds.) ECCV 2020. LNCS, vol. 12367, pp. 68–83. Springer, Cham (2020). https://doi.org/10.1007/978-3-030-58542-6_5
17. Serai, S.D.: Basics of magnetic resonance imaging and quantitative parameters T1, T2, T2*, T1rho and diffusion-weighted imaging. Pediatr. Radiol. **52**(2), 217–227 (2022)
18. Shakur, A., Lee, J.Y.J., Freeman, S.: An update on the role of MRI in treatment stratification of patients with cervical cancer. Cancers **15**(20), 5105 (2023)
19. Siegel, R.L., Miller, K.D., Wagle, N.S., Jemal, A., et al.: Cancer statistics, 2023. CA Cancer J. Clin. **73**(1), 17–48 (2023)
20. Su, Z., Yao, K., Yang, X., Huang, K., Wang, Q., Sun, J.: Rethinking data augmentation for single-source domain generalization in medical image segmentation. In: Proceedings of the AAAI Conference on Artificial Intelligence, vol. 37, pp. 2366–2374 (2023)
21. Wang, J., et al.: Generalizing to unseen domains: a survey on domain generalization. IEEE Trans. Knowl. Data Eng. (2022)
22. Wilson, G., Cook, D.J.: A survey of unsupervised deep domain adaptation. ACM Trans. Intell. Syst. Technol. (TIST) **11**(5), 1–46 (2020)
23. Xia, C., et al.: Cancer statistics in china and united states, 2022: profiles, trends, and determinants. Chin. Med. J. **135**(05), 584–590 (2022). https://doi.org/10.1097/CM9.0000000000002108
24. Xu, Y., Xie, S., Reynolds, M., Ragoza, M., Gong, M., Batmanghelich, K.: Adversarial consistency for single domain generalization in medical image segmentation. In: Wang, L., Dou, Q., Fletcher, P.T., Speidel, S., Li, S. (eds.) MICCAI 2022. LNCS, vol. 13437, pp. 671–681. Springer, Cham (2022). https://doi.org/10.1007/978-3-031-16449-1_64
25. Yoon, J.S., Oh, K., Shin, Y., Mazurowski, M.A., Suk, H.I.: Domain generalization for medical image analysis: a survey. arXiv preprint arXiv:2310.08598 (2023)
26. Zhou, K., Liu, Z., Qiao, Y., Xiang, T., Loy, C.C.: Domain generalization: a survey. IEEE Trans. Pattern Anal. Mach. Intell. **45**(4), 4396–4415 (2022)
27. Zhou, K., Yang, Y., Qiao, Y., Xiang, T.: Domain generalization with MixStyle. In: International Conference on Learning Representations (2021). https://openreview.net/forum?id=6xHJ37MVxxp
28. Zhou, Z., Qi, L., Yang, X., Ni, D., Shi, Y.: Generalizable cross-modality medical image segmentation via style augmentation and dual normalization. In: Proceedings of the IEEE/CVF Conference on Computer Vision and Pattern Recognition, pp. 20856–20865 (2022)
29. Zhu, L., Ji, D., Zhu, S., Gan, W., Wu, W., Yan, J.: Learning statistical texture for semantic segmentation. In: Proceedings of the IEEE/CVF Conference on Computer Vision and Pattern Recognition, pp. 12537–12546 (2021)

PANDA: Pneumonitis Anomaly Detection Using Attention U-Net

Amgad Muneer[1], Eman Showkatian[1], Mehmet Altan[3], Ajay Sheshadri[2], and Jia Wu[1,3(✉)]

[1] Department of Imaging Physics, MD Anderson Cancer Center, Houston, TX, USA
jwu11@mdanderson.org
[2] Departments of Pulmonary Medicine, MD Anderson Cancer Center, Houston, TX, USA
[3] Department of Thoracic/Head and Neck Medical Oncology, MD Anderson Cancer Center, Houston, TX, USA

Abstract. Immune checkpoint inhibitors (ICIs) are a cornerstone of modern onco-logical treatments, particularly in the management of various cancers through immunotherapy. Despite their clinical success, ICIs are often associated with several immune-related adverse events (irAEs), among which pneumonitis is particularly significant due to its potential severity. Accurately identifying patients at high-risk of developing ICI-induced pneumonitis remains a critical challenge in lung cancer patient management. Early detection and precise differentiation are essential for timely and appropriate therapeutic interventions, which can significantly alter patient outcomes. We developed the PANDA (Pneumonitis ANomaly Detection using AttentionU-Net) model to address this challenge, leveraging advanced deep learning techniques to improve the early predicting of ICI-induced pneumonitis. Baseline CT scans from 348 cases (33 pneumonitis cases) patients undergoing ICI therapy were analyzed to train and validate the model. The PANDA model utilizes the Attention U-Net architecture, incorporating attention mechanisms to enhance feature extraction and anomaly detection capabilities. Data augmentation techniques, including brightness normalization and pixel shuffling, were applied to improve model robustness. The model was trained on normal cases using an autoencoder-based method with anomaly detection through mean squared error (MSE) distribution, followed by testing on pneumonitis cases. The PANDA model demonstrated superior performance, achieving a precision of 0.76, sensitivity of 0.79, specificity of 0.79, F1-score of 0.78, AUC of 0.85 and a Precision-Recall AUC of 0.82. These results significantly outperform traditional models, including clinical and radiomics approaches. The clinical model, for instance, achieved a precision of 0.75, sensitivity of 0.67, specificity of 0.73, F1-score of 0.76, AUC of 0.69 and a precision-recall AUC of 0.76. The classical radiomics model showed improvements over the clinical model, with a precision of 0.81, sensitivity of 0.72, specificity of 0.80, F1-score of 0.76, AUC of 0.70 and a precision-recall AUC of 0.79, but still fell short of the PANDA model's performance. These comparisons emphasize the enhanced predictive capacity of the deep learning approach, significantly outperforming traditional models.

A. Muneer and E. Showkatian—Contributed equally

© The Author(s), under exclusive license to Springer Nature Switzerland AG 2025
J. Wu et al. (Eds.): CMMCA 2024, LNCS 15181, pp. 80–89, 2025.
https://doi.org/10.1007/978-3-031-73360-4_9

Keywords: Interstitial Lung Abnormalities · Pneumonitis · Immune Checkpoint Inhibitors · Deep Learning · Lung Cancer · Computed tomography

1 Introduction

The advent of immune checkpoint inhibitors (ICIs) has revolutionized the treatment landscape for various cancers, including lung cancer [1–6]. Despite their clinical success, ICIs are associated with a range of immune-related adverse events, with pneumonitis being one of the most serious complications [7, 8]. Early prediction of ICI-induced pneumonitis is critical for timely intervention and improving patient outcomes [9, 10]. However, the subtle and heterogeneous nature of Interstitial Lung Abnormalities (ILA) on imaging poses a significant challenge for radiologists [11, 12].

Predicting immune checkpoint inhibitor-induced pneumonitis (ICI-pneumonitis) from baseline CT scans is of paramount importance as it can significantly enhance clinical decision-making and patient management [11]. Early identification of at-risk patients can lead to timely interventions, minimizing morbidity and potentially saving lives [13]. Furthermore, understanding imaging biomarkers for pneumonitis can contribute to the broader knowledge of immune-related adverse events, guiding future therapeutic strategies and monitoring protocols [14, 15].

Despite advances in medical imaging and artificial intelligence, several gaps remain in the prediction of ICI-pneumonitis. Existing models are often limited by small datasets and lack generalizability [16, 17]. Most studies focus on symptomatic patients or follow-up scans rather than leveraging baseline scans for early prediction. Additionally, the intricate and subtle imaging features associated with pneumonitis are challenging to identify and interpret, requiring advanced deep learning techniques [18]. The motivation for this research stems from the need to improve the early prediction of ICI-pneumonitis, ultimately enhancing patient outcomes. By utilizing advanced deep learning models, specifically autoencoder, which have demonstrated superior performance in capturing complex spatial relationships in medical images and anomaly detection, we aim to overcome the limitations of traditional approaches such radiomics or clinical models. Autoencoders offer a more efficient way to abstract the CT scans, potentially uncovering subtle biomarkers indicative of pneumonitis risk.

In literature, several studies have explored the application of deep learning in medical imaging, with notable successes in tumor detection, segmentation, and classification. Recent advancements in autoencoders have shown promise in various imaging tasks, outperforming Convolutional Neural Networks (CNNs) in certain scenarios due to their ability to model long-range dependencies and spatial hierarchies. Specific to ICI-pneumonitis, previous works have primarily relied on CNN-based, ML-based models or radiomic features, with varying degrees of success [19–24]. However, the predictive power of these models remains limited by the complexity of pneumonitis presentation and the heterogeneity of patient populations. Our study addresses these limitations by utilizing an autoencoder-based deep learning approach with a 3D Res-Unet50 architecture, demonstrating superior performance in predicting ICI-induced pneumonitis and highlighting the potential for improved patient outcomes through early prediction and precise differentiation.

2 Methods

Figure 1 illustrates the workflow of the PANDA (Pneumonitis ANomaly Detection using AttentionU-Net) model, designed for the early prediction of risk to develop ICI-induced pneumonitis from baseline CT scans in lung cancer patients. The process begins with the acquisition of baseline CT scans from lung cancer patients. The CT images are pre-processed to isolate the lung region, using a lung segmentation algorithm [25]. This step ensures that the model focuses on the relevant anatomical structures. From the segmented lung regions, random samples are extracted, and a lung windowing technique is applied to enhance the visibility of lung tissue structures. The core of the PANDA model is an encoder-decoder network based on the Attention U-Net architecture. The encoder path consists of several convolutional blocks, each followed by max pooling layers to progressively downsample the feature maps and capture hierarchical features. Each block includes 3 × 3 convolutional layers with ReLU activation, batch normalization, and dropout for regularization. At the bottleneck, the deepest layer of the network, the feature maps are highly abstracted. The decoder path upsamples the feature maps using transposed convolutions and concatenates them with corresponding encoder features via skip connections. This process helps in retaining spatial information and improving localization accuracy. The attention modules are incorporated at various stages to enhance the model's focus on relevant features, reducing the impact of irrelevant background information.

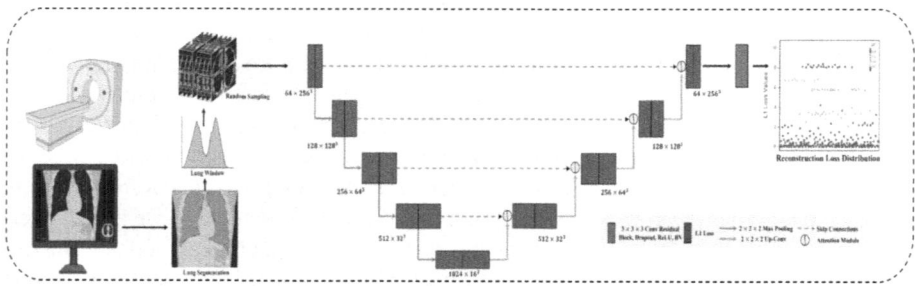

Fig. 1. Workflow of the PANDA model for early detection of ICI-induced pneumonitis.

For the reconstruction loss calculation, PANDA employs an autoencoder-based approach, where the CT images are reconstructed, and the reconstruction loss is computed. This loss distribution is used to detect anomalies indicative of pneumonitis. A high reconstruction loss suggests the presence of anomalies that the model has not encountered during training on normal cases. The final output of the model is a reconstruction loss distribution, where higher loss values indicate potential pneumonitis cases. This output assists in differentiating between normal and abnormal cases, facilitating early intervention and appropriate therapeutic measures.

2.1 Study Design and Patient Cohorts

This retrospective modeling study utilized in-house baseline CT images, collected from the IntelliSpace PACS by Philips, served as the foundational dataset for model development and validation with a total cohort of 348. Patients with NSCLC who were treated with ICI alone or in combination with chemotherapy were identified from the MD Anderson GEMINI database, which includes some clinical information such as sex, race, smoking status, cough at the baseline, fever at the baseline, shortness of breath at baseline. These 6 clinical factors were used to build the clinical model. In the clinical and radiomics model, we have used 15 non-pneumonitis and 18 pneumonitis cases for testing. For PANDA-based deep learning model, we used 39 non-pneumonitis and 33 pneumonitis cases for testing purposes.

3 Results and Analysis

In this section, we present and analyze the results of our PANDA deep learning model designed to predict immune checkpoint inhibitor (ICI)-induced pneumonitis from baseline CT scans in lung cancer patients. Our model, employing a 3D attention U-Net architecture and etc and an autoencoder-based feature extraction method, demonstrated significant improvements in predictive performance compared to traditional clinical and radiomics models.

The performance metrics of the three models: clinical, radiomics and PANDA are compared in Table 1.. This comparison reveals the superior performance of our proposed PANDA model across multiple evaluation criteria, indicating its potential for accurately predicting ICI-induced pneumonitis from baseline CT scans. As shown in Table 1., the PANDA model achieved the highest AUC of 82%, surpassing the clinical model (67%) and radiomics model (72%).

Table 1. Benchmarking PANDA against other traditional models' performance.

Model	Precision	Sensitivity	Specificity	F1 Score	AUC	Precision-Recall AUC
Clinical	0.75	0.67	0.73	0.76	0.69	0.76
Radiomics	0.81	0.72	0.80	0.76	0.70	0.79
PANDA	0.76	0.79	0.79	0.78	0.85	0.82

These performance metrics of the clinical, radiomics, and PANDA models are compared in Fig. 2. It provides a comprehensive evaluation of the models based on precision, sensitivity, specificity, F1 score, and precision-recall AUC. The clinical model, as depicted in Fig. 2, demonstrates the lowest performance among the three models across most metrics. It achieved a precision of 0.75, sensitivity of 0.67, specificity of 0.73, F1 score of 0.76, AUC of 0.69 and precision-recall AUC of 0.76. These results indicate that while the clinical model can identify pneumonitis cases to some extent, its overall predictive accuracy is limited.

The radiomics model shows an improvement over the clinical model, with better performance across all metrics. It achieved a precision of 0.81, sensitivity of 0.72, specificity of 0.80, F1 score of 0.76, AUC of 0.70 and precision-recall AUC of 0.79. These metrics highlight the radiomics model's enhanced capability in accurately identifying pneumonitis cases through quantitative imaging features. The PANDA model, which leverages the AttentionU-Net architecture, exhibits the highest performance across all metrics. It achieved a precision of 0.76, sensitivity of 0.79, specificity of 0.79, F1 score of 0.78, AUC of 0.85 and precision-recall AUC of 0.82. These results emphasize the PANDA model's superior ability to balance precision and recall, ensuring more accurate and reliable detection of pneumonitis cases compared to the clinical and radiomics models. Overall, the PANDA model demonstrates significant improvements in predictive performance, making it a robust tool for early detection of pneumonitis. Its higher precision-recall AUC indicates better handling of imbalanced data, reducing false positives while maintaining high recall rates. This superior AUC reinforces the model's robustness and its potential utility in clinical practice for the reliable detection of pneumonitis.

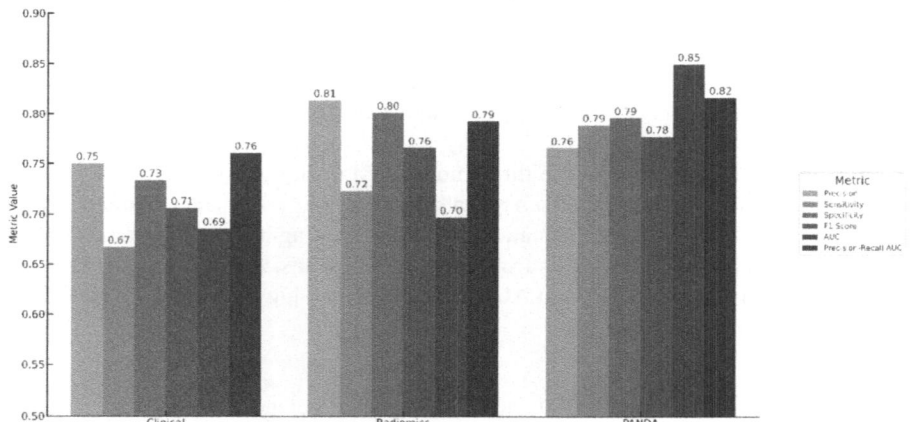

Fig. 2. Comparison of model performance metrics across different models for predicting ICI-induced pneumonitis from baseline CT scans.

Figure 3 provides a comparative evaluation of the performance of the Clinical, Radiomics, and PANDA models through ROC (Receiver Operating Characteristic) and Precision-Recall (PR) curves. The ROC curves plot the true positive rate (sensitivity) against the false positive rate (1-specificity) for the three models, with the Area Under the Curve (AUC) serving as a key performance indicator (Fig. 3a). The ROC curve for the clinical model shows an AUC of 0.69, indicating a limited ability to distinguish between pneumonitis and non-pneumonitis cases based solely on clinical assessments. The radiomics model slightly improves upon the clinical model, achieving an AUC of 0.70. This suggests that while the incorporation of quantitative imaging features enhances predictive capability, it remains inadequate for reliable pneumonitis detection. The PANDA model demonstrates the highest AUC of 0.85, highlighting its superior discriminative power. The enhanced architecture of the PANDA model allows for better differentiation between true positive and false positive cases, making it a more reliable tool for early detection of pneumonitis.

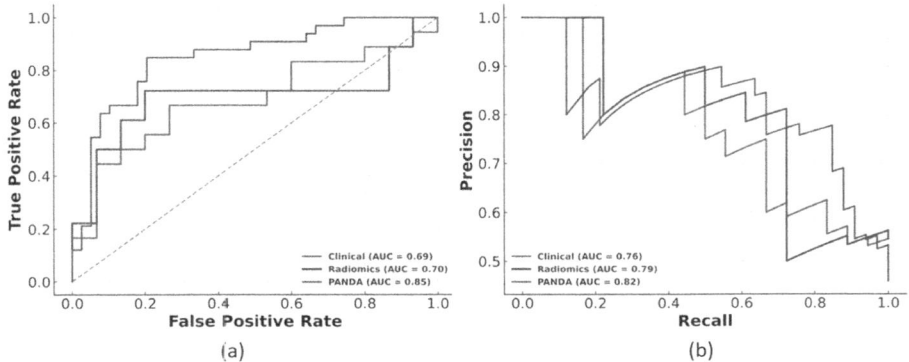

Fig. 3. (a) ROC curves for different models. The PANDA model demonstrates the highest AUC of 0.85, indicating superior discriminative ability. (b) Precision-Recall curves for clinical, radiomics, and panda models. The PANDA model again outperforms with the highest AUC of 0.82, reflecting its robust predictive performance.

The PR curves provide a more detailed view of the models' performance, especially important in imbalanced datasets common in medical diagnostics. The curves plot precision (positive predictive value) against recall (sensitivity), with the AUC indicating the overall balance between these metrics. The PR curve for the clinical model shows an AUC of 0.76, reflecting a relatively low balance between precision and recall. This model tends to generate a higher number of false positives, reducing its overall reliability. The radiomics model achieves a PR AUC of 0.79, demonstrating an improvement in balancing precision and recall compared to the clinical model. However, it still falls short in maintaining high precision and recall simultaneously. The PANDA model excels with the highest PR AUC of 0.82 (Fig. 3b). This indicates its superior capability to maintain high precision and recall, ensuring fewer false positives and more accurate detection of true pneumonitis cases. The advanced AttentionU-Net architecture contributes to this model's robust performance, making it a highly effective tool for clinical application.

The PANDA model's performance, as depicted in both the ROC and PR curves, clearly surpasses that of the clinical and radiomics models. Its higher AUC values (0.85 for ROC and 0.82 for PR) underscore its enhanced discriminative ability and precision-recall balance. These metrics validate PANDA's effectiveness in accurately identifying pneumonitis cases while minimizing false positives, a critical aspect for improving patient outcomes. The use of the AttentionU-Net architecture in PANDA significantly contributes to its superior performance, leveraging advanced deep learning techniques to capture subtle anomalies in baseline CT scans.

Additionally, Fig. 4 presents the confusion matrices for the clinical, radiomics, and PANDA models. These matrices provide a detailed breakdown of the models' performance in terms of true positives, true negatives, false positives, and false negatives, offering insights into their predictive accuracy. The comparison of these confusion matrices underscores the PANDA model's enhanced performance. The significant increase in true positives and true negatives, coupled with the reduction in false positives and false negatives, validates the model's robustness and reliability in clinical applications. Lastly, by leveraging the AttentionU-Net architecture, the PANDA model successfully captures subtle anomalies in baseline CT scans, leading to more accurate and early detection of pneumonitis.

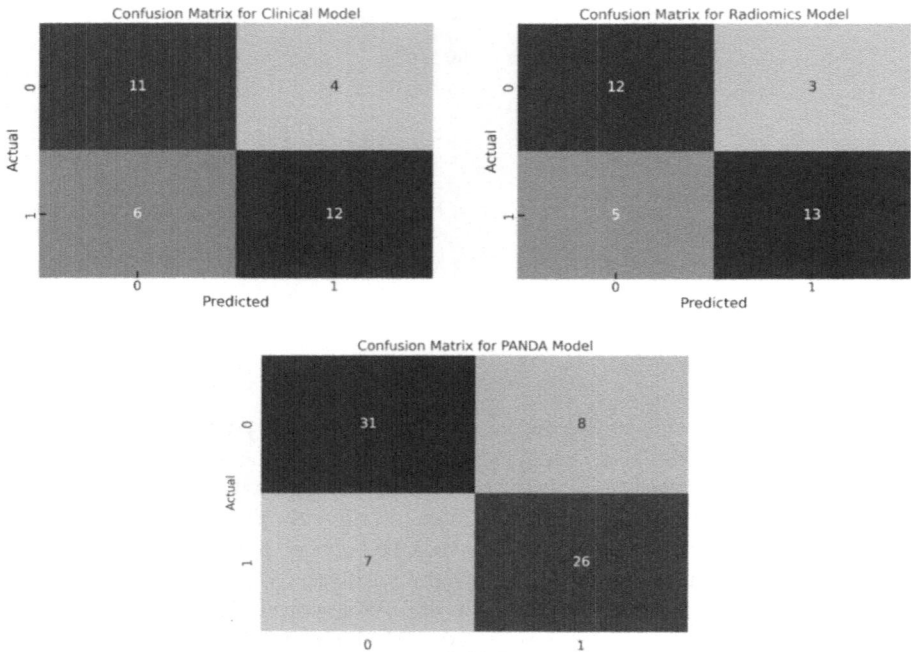

Fig. 4. Comparison of confusion matrices for different prediction models, where 0 represent non-pneumonitis and 1 represent pneumonitis.

Figure 5 showcases some challenging cases of pneumonitis identified by our in-house radiologist in baseline CT scans of lung cancer patients undergoing immune checkpoint inhibitor therapy. Figure 5a The CT scan reveals pneumonitis in the lower left lung, with an enlarged view showing the specific inflamed region. Figure 5b highlights pneumonitis in the lower right lung, with a close-up of the affected area demonstrating characteristic inflammation. Figure 5c shows multiple regions in both the left and right lungs are affected by pneumonitis, as shown in the zoomed-in views of the highlighted areas. Figure 5d shows a significant pneumonitis manifestation is visible in the upper left lung, with the enlarged section clearly depicting the inflamed lung tissue.

These examples (Fig. 5) illustrate the variability and complexity of pneumonitis presentations, emphasizing the need for advanced predication methods like the PANDA model to accurately identify and differentiate such cases.

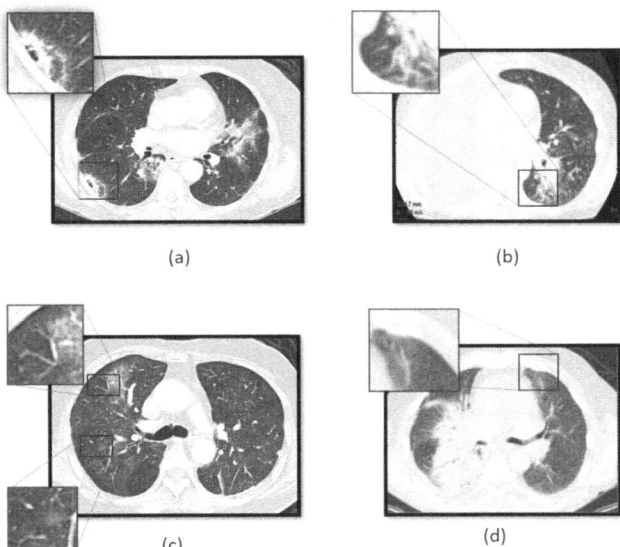

(a)   (b)

(c)   (d)

Fig. 5. Visualization of challenging pneumonitis cases in baseline CT scans of lung cancer patients undergoing ICI therapy. Each sub-figure (a, b, c, and d) highlights specific regions of pneumonitis in the lungs, with zoomed-in views to better illustrate the anomalies. These cases demonstrate the variability and complexity of pneumonitis manifestations, underscoring the necessity for advanced detection models like PANDA for accurate diagnosis and management.

4 Conclusion

In conclusion, our study demonstrates that the PANDA model significantly improves the prediction of immune checkpoint inhibitor-induced pneumonitis from baseline CT scans in lung cancer patients. The PANDA model, utilizing the advanced AttentionU-Net architecture, achieved high performance metrics. These results clearly surpass the performance of traditional models, including clinical and radiomics approaches.

The PANDA model's superior accuracy and balanced precision-recall performance highlight its potential as a valuable tool for the early detection and differentiation of ICI-induced pneumonitis. This advancement is crucial for improving patient outcomes, as pneumonitis is a significant and potentially severe immune-related adverse event in ICI therapy. Our findings highlight the limitations of traditional models, with the clinical model showing an accuracy of ~70% and an AUC of 69%. Although the radiomics models showed improvements, they did not achieve the predictive capacity of the PANDA model.

The developed deep learning-based PANDA model effectively differentiates between those likely or unlikely to develop ICI-induced pneumonitis. By integrating this model into clinical workflows, it is possible to significantly improve decision-making processes, enhance patient monitoring, and potentially reduce both the incidence and severity of pneumonitis. These improvements could lead to better patient management strategies and outcomes, highlighting the importance of advanced imaging analytics in contemporary medical practice. This study not only fills a crucial gap in early pneumonitis detection but also sets a precedent for the application of advanced machine learning techniques in the prediction and management of irAEs.

References

1. Huang, Z., et al.: First-line immune-checkpoint inhibitors in non-small cell lung cancer: current landscape and future progress. Front. Pharmacol. **11**, 578091 (2020)
2. Bianco, A., D'Agnano, V., Matera, M.G., Della Gravara, L., Perrotta, F., Rocco, D.: Immune checkpoint inhibitors: a new landscape for extensive stage small cell lung cancer treatment. Expert Rev. Respir. Med. **15**(11), 1415–1425 (2021)
3. Zhou, F., Qiao, M., Zhou, C.: The cutting-edge progress of immune-checkpoint blockade in lung cancer. Cell. Mol. Immunol. **18**(2), 279–293 (2021)
4. Mamdani, H., Matosevic, S., Khalid, A.B., Durm, G., Jalal, S.I.: Immunotherapy in lung cancer: current landscape and future directions. Front. Immunol. **13**, 823618 (2022)
5. Pasello, G., et al.: Real world data in the era of Immune Checkpoint Inhibitors (ICIs): increasing evidence and future applications in lung cancer. Cancer Treat. Rev. **87**, 102031 (2020)
6. Genova, C., et al.: Therapeutic implications of tumor microenvironment in lung cancer: focus on immune checkpoint blockade. Front. Immunol. **12**, 799455 (2022)
7. Grangeon, M., et al.: Association between immune-related adverse events and efficacy of immune checkpoint inhibitors in non–small-cell lung cancer. Clin. Lung Cancer **20**(3), 201–207 (2019)
8. Isono, T., et al.: Outcome and risk factor of immune-related adverse events and pneumonitis in patients with advanced or postoperative recurrent non-small cell lung cancer treated with immune checkpoint inhibitors. Thorac. Cancer **12**(2), 153–164 (2021)
9. Kalisz, K.R., Ramaiya, N.H., Laukamp, K.R., Gupta, A.: Immune checkpoint inhibitor therapy–related pneumonitis: patterns and management. Radiographics **39**(7), 1923–1937 (2019)
10. Özdemir, B.C., et al.: Multidisciplinary recommendations for essential baseline functional and laboratory tests to facilitate early diagnosis and management of immune-related adverse events among cancer patients. Cancer Immunol. Immunother. **72**(7), 1991–2001 (2023)
11. Rea, G., et al.: The unveiled triad: clinical, radiological and pathological insights into hypersensitivity pneumonitis. J. Clin. Med. **13**(3), 797 (2024)
12. Dabiri, M., Jehangir, M., Khoshpouri, P., Chalian, H.: Hypersensitivity pneumonitis: a pictorial review based on the new ATS/JRS/ALAT clinical practice guideline for radiologists and pulmonologists. Diagnostics **12**(11), 2874 (2022)
13. McGaughey, J., O'Halloran, P., Porter, S., Blackwood, B.: Early warning systems and rapid response to the deteriorating patient in hospital: a systematic realist review. J. Adv. Nurs. **73**(12), 2877–2891 (2017)
14. Zhang, Q., Tang, L., Zhou, Y., He, W., Li, W.: Immune checkpoint inhibitor-associated pneumonitis in non-small cell lung cancer: current understanding in characteristics, diagnosis, and management. Front. Immunol. **12**, 663986 (2021)
15. Lin, M.X., Zang, D., Liu, C.G., Han, X., Chen, J.: Immune checkpoint inhibitor-related pneumonitis: research advances in prediction and management. Front. Immunol. **15**, 1266850 (2024)
16. Maleki, F., Ovens, K., Gupta, R., Reinhold, C., Spatz, A., Forghani, R.: Generalizability of machine learning models: quantitative evaluation of three methodological pitfalls. Radiol. Artif. Intell. **5**(1), e220028 (2022)

17. Yu, H., et al.: Machine learning to build and validate a model for radiation pneumonitis prediction in patients with non–small cell lung cancer. Clin. Cancer Res. **25**(14), 4343–4350 (2019)

18. Walsh, S.L., et al.: Role of imaging in progressive-fibrosing interstitial lung diseases. Eur. Respir. Rev. **27**(150) (2018)

19. Yang, L., Cui, H., Duan, Y., Yao, Y., Zou, B., Wang, L.: Radiotherapy-immunotherapy related pneumonitis prediction from pre-treatment CT using a deep graph-based integrative model (2022)

20. Zhou, Y., et al.: The application of artificial intelligence and radiomics in lung cancer. Precis. Clin. Med. **3**(3), 214–227 (2020)

21. Chen, X., et al.: Radiation versus immune checkpoint inhibitor associated pneumonitis: distinct radiologic morphologies. Oncologist **26**(10), e1822–e1832 (2021)

22. Cheng, M., et al.: Deep learning for predicting the risk of immune checkpoint inhibitor-related pneumonitis in lung cancer. Clin. Radiol. **78**(5), e377–e385 (2023)

23. Chen, X., et al.: CT radiomics and machine learning for distinguishing radiotherapy vs. immune checkpoint inhibitor-induced pneumonitis in non-small cell lung cancer patients. Int. J. Radiat. Oncol. Biol. Phys. **108**(3), S163 (2020)

24. Cheng, J., et al.: Differentiation between immune checkpoint inhibitor-related and radiation pneumonitis in lung cancer by CT radiomics and machine learning. Med. Phys. **49**(3), 1547–1558 (2022)

25. Isensee, F., Jaeger, P.F., Kohl, S.A., Petersen, J., Maier-Hein, K.H.: NnU-Net: a self-configuring method for deep learning-based biomedical image segmentation. Nat. Methods **18**(2), 203–211 (2021)

Estimating the Average Treatment Effect Using Weighting Methods in Lung Cancer Immunotherapy

Maliazurina B. Saad[1] (ID), Qasem Al-Tashi[1] (ID), Lingzhi Hong[2] (ID), Wentao Li[1] (ID), Shenduo Li[4] (ID), John V. Heymach[2] (ID), Yanyan Lou[4] (ID), Natalie I. Vokes[2,3] (ID), Jianjun Zhang[2,3] (ID), and Jia Wu[1,2(✉)] (ID)

[1] Department of Imaging Physics, MD Anderson Cancer Center, Houston, TX, USA
jwu11@mdanderson.org
[2] Department of Thoracic/Head and Neck Medical Oncology, MD Anderson Cancer Center, Houston, TX, USA
[3] Department of Genomic Medicine, MD Anderson Cancer Center, Houston, TX, USA
[4] Department of Hematology and Oncology, Mayo Clinic, Jacksonville, FL, USA

Abstract. Traditionally, identifying predictive biomarkers for treatment efficacy involves evaluating treatment-marker interactions through regression models considering clinical outcomes. This study seeks optimal personalized treatment strategies, known as individualized treatment rules (ITRs) through innovative approach utilizing weighting method and formulation of personalized treatment scoring. Integrating two scoring methods, (linear vs. non-linear) we aim to elucidate clinicogenomic indicators predictive of treatment efficacy. Emphasis is placed on identifying patients at elevated risk for early progression and determining their optimal treatment choice between immune checkpoint inhibitor-monotherapy (ICI-Mono) and ICI-Chemotherapy (ICI-Chemo). A total of 408 non-small cell lung cancer (NSCLC) patients, from MD Anderson and Mayo Clinic were enrolled. Performance was evaluated as average treatment effect of weighted risk reduction for 3-months progression between subgroup of patients who were treated according to vs. against model's recommendation. The non-linear scoring method shows better performance comparing to the linear scoring method (overall risk reduction: -25.4% vs. -15.5% in training and -14.3 vs. -9.6% in testing cohort). Tobacco exposure and lung adenocarcinoma significantly influences outcomes in the ICI-Mono while stage-IVB and KRAS mutated gene associated with great effect from ICI-Chemo. These findings offer valuable insights for seamlessly integrating precision medicine into real-world clinical scenarios.

Keywords: average treatment effect · weighting method · immune-checkpoint inhibitors

1 Introduction

The benefits of treatments vary significantly among different patient subgroups. Aligning patients with the most effective treatments enhances treatment efficacy [1]. For example, immune checkpoint inhibitors (ICIs) have transformed non-small cell lung cancer

© The Author(s), under exclusive license to Springer Nature Switzerland AG 2025
J. Wu et al. (Eds.): CMMCA 2024, LNCS 15181, pp. 90–98, 2025.
https://doi.org/10.1007/978-3-031-73360-4_10

(NSCLC) treatment, but only a small percentage of patients experience long-term disease control [2]. Research has focused on biomarker-driven strategies, leading to approvals for first-line ICI plus chemotherapy (ICI-Chemo) and ICI monotherapy (ICI-Mono). However, determining which patients should receive ICI-Chemo or ICI-Mono is still unclear due to the lack of direct comparisons in previous trials [3]. Matching patients with appropriate treatments based on their characteristics is crucial [4].

There has been substantial effort in the statistics and machine learning community to develop methods for determining the optimal treatment for patients. This involves identifying subgroups based on treatment effect heterogeneity. Recent methods include interaction trees [5], differential effect search [6], virtual twins [7], and others [8–11]. Improving treatment selection involves using baseline covariates to rank or score individualized treatment effects (ITEs). These covariates can be treatment-moderating (impacting treatment effect) or prognostic (impacting outcomes regardless of treatment).

Subgroup identification methods range from ad hoc techniques to model-dependent approaches, relying on various assumptions about treatment effects. Many methods use treatment difference as the primary measure for summarizing ITE, but the chosen metric can impact analyses and inferences. While estimating subgroups based on patient characteristics is well-studied, evaluating treatment effects within these subgroups is also crucial and challenging. In this study we extend the weighting approach by adopting two scoring models to determine optimal immunotherapy plans for NSCLC patients. Our objectives are to assess the impact of adding chemotherapy on early progression outcomes in NSCLC patients receiving ICI therapy and to explore the association of clinic-genomic features with ICI outcomes to guide appropriate treatment selection.

2 Methods

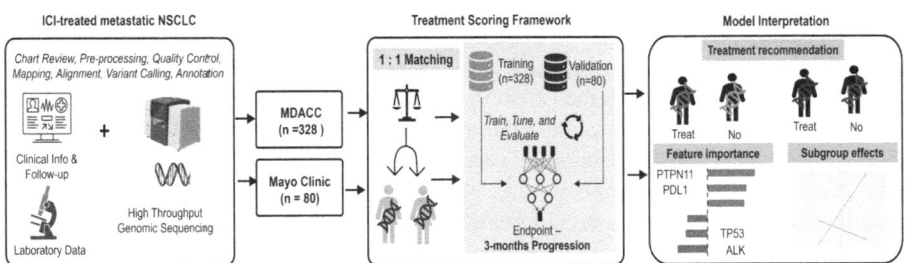

Fig. 1. Overview of the overall pipeline

2.1 General Study Design

Figure 1 illustrates the overall framework used in this study. First, the clinical ($n = 9$) and molecular features ($n = 31$) of the MDACC cohort were curated, and then a propensity score matching was calculated to mitigate the patient heterogeneity of real-world data, resulting in a matched cohort (328 patients matched out of 750 patients) that was utilized for fine-tuning model hyperparameters. We then validated the trained model on an external cohort from Mayo clinic (n = 80). Finally, we addressed the clinical values of the estimated treatment effect.

2.2 Potential Outcome Framework

Without loss of generality, according to Rubin et al. [12] we can represent the expected outcome (Y) given the treatment (T) and initial covariates (X) as $E[Y|T, X] = \emptyset(X) + T \times \Delta(X)/2$, where $\emptyset(X)$ is a function that represents the main prognostic effect and can be calculated as $E[Y|T = 1, X] + E[Y|T = 0, X]$ and $\Delta(X)$ indicates the treatment effect which can be expressed as $E[Y|T = 1, X] - E[Y|T = 0, X]$. Hence, developing a model for $(Y|T, X)$ involves constructing functions for both $\emptyset(X)$ and $\Delta(X)$ based on the covariates. Variables used in constructing $\emptyset(X)$ are referred to as prognostic variables, while those used in constructing $\Delta(X)$ are called treatment moderators [13, 14].

The endpoint in this study was progression at 3 months (denoted as Y(1)) or no progression at 3 months (denoted as Y(0)). Two types of treatment involves: ICI-Chemo, denoted as $T = 1$, or ICI-Mono denoted as $T = 0$. Additionally, we assumed that only a single treatment outcome, either Y(1) or Y(0), can be observed per patient. We also assumed that T is not dependent on (Y(1), Y(0)) [12]. To assign treatment, we assumed that the probability of receiving treatment, given certain covariates X, is represented by the propensity score $\pi(X)$, calculated as $\pi(Xi) = Pr(T = 1|X)$. In randomize trials, this score is typically known and not influenced by X, but in observational studies, it needs to be estimated. The data we observe is represented by n independent and identically distributed copies of (Y, T, X), denoted as $\{(Yi, Ti, Xi), i = 1,\dots,\}$.

2.3 Benefit Score Estimation

The weighting subgroup method [4, 15] was utilized to develop a personalized benefit scoring system $f(X)$ based on the covariates X, in which personalized treatment will be suggested for individual patients using $f(X)$. A benefit score is any function $f(X)$ that meets two criteria: (i) it shows the extent to which patients benefit from certain treatment and (ii) it has meaningful cut-point value c, such that for a given level of covariates X, $f(X) < c$ indicates that ICI-Chemo is more effective than ICI-Mono (i.e., $\Delta(X) < 0$), and $f(X) \geq c$ indicates the opposite (i.e., $\Delta(X) \geq c$). Here, $\Delta(X)$ can serve as a benefit score, as it represents the expected benefit a patient will derive from ICI-Chemo in terms of their outcome. Hence, estimating $\Delta(X)$ or its sign enables optimal treatment recommendation for different patient subgroups. By definition, $\Delta(X)$ can also be used to rank patients based on the magnitude of treatment effect [4, 15].

Another measure of interest is ITR, a function that maps patient covariates to the treatment decision, $d(X):X \to T$. Optimal ITRs aim to maximize the average outcomes across the population by making treatment decisions for patients in a way that maximizes the value function $(d) = Ed(Y) = YdPd$ where Pd is the distribution of (Y, T, X), given $T = d(X)$. As a result, $\Delta(X)$ can be used to develop optimal ITRs. Specifically, sign $\{f(X)\}$ is considered as optimal ITRs [4, 15]. A convex loss function $(y; v)$ can be used to estimate benefit scores, for example a squared error loss, $M(y; v) = (y - v)^2$. Chen et al. [15] originally proposed that $M(y; v)$ should meet two conditions. First, $M(y; v)$

$= \partial M(y; v)/\partial v =$ is increasing in v for every fixed y. Second, $v(y; 0)$ is monotone in y. These conditions are adequate for Fisher consistent subgroup identification, but they are not mandatory [4].

2.4 Weighting Method for Subgroup Identification

The weighting method represents a versatile approach for estimating $\Delta(X)$ as it does not mandate the specification of a complete outcome regression model. Rather, it prioritizes the direct estimation of $\Delta(X)$, eliminating the necessity for a detailed outcome regression model. A significant advantage of the weighting method is that, even when complete outcome regression models are employed, the validity of the resulting estimators remains unaffected by potential misspecifications in the said models. Assuming a sample size of n patients, the objective of the weighting method is to estimate $\Delta(X)$ by minimizing the given objective function with respect to $f(X)$ [4, 15]:

$$L_W(f) = \frac{1}{n} \sum_{i=1}^{n} \frac{M\{Y_i, T_i \times f(X_i)\}}{T_i \pi(X_i) + (1 - T_i)/2} \tag{1}$$

where W represents the method of weighting and $\pi(X_i) = Pr(T = 1|X)$ is the propensity score function that is computed previously. The estimator of weighting is then $fW = argminf\ L(f)$. The corresponding population level weighting estimator is the minimizer of [4, 15]:

$$l_W(f, x) = E\left[\frac{M(Y, T \times f(x))}{T\pi(x) + (1 - T)/2}|X = x\right], \tag{2}$$

with respect to f, where W denotes the method of weighting. This method is applicable even if the complete outcome regression model is not specified, as the inverse weights ensure that the interactions between T and $f(X)$ are not correlated with the main effects of $\emptyset(X)$. The benefit score estimated using the weighting method, represented by $\hat{f}_W$, can be used to estimate $\Delta(X)$ under various loss functions. While $\hat{f}_W(.)$ may not be direct estimator of $\Delta(X.)$, the zero point has a significant meaning and can be employed as a threshold to identify subgroups. For instance, if smaller outcomes are preferred, patients with covariates x satisfying $f_W(x) < 0$ should generally experience better outcomes with treatment than without it on average. To be precise, let the population estimators be denoted as [4, 15]:

$$f_{W0}(x) = argmin_f\{l_W(f, x)\}, \tag{3}$$

For patients with a negative benefit score ($f_{W0}(x) < 0$) under the weighting method and the two aforementioned conditions of M, the expected utility of $Y^{(0)}$ given $X = x$ is greater than the expected utility of $Y^{(1)}$ given $X = x$ and denoted as $E\{U(Y^{(0)})|X = x\} > E\{U(Y^{(1)})|X = x\}$ where $U(y) = \partial M(y; v)/\partial v|_{v=0}$ and for those with a positive benefit score, the opposite is true. Therefore, the optimal decision rules for mapping patient covariates X to treatment decision T is $d_{W0}(X) = sign(f_{W0}(x))$. It should be noted that the treatment assignment decisions are based on the individual treatment effects, although the overall cutoff value is 0 [4, 15]. Moreover, the benefit scores can indicate the extent of the individual treatment effect and can be utilized to rank patients based on the effectiveness of the treatment. For instance, if $M(y; v) = (y - v)^2$ is utilized, then [4, 15]:

$$2f_{W0}(x) = E\left(Y^{(0)}|X = x\right) - E\left(Y^{(1)}|X = x\right) = \Delta(X) \tag{4}$$

In this work, we illustrated the benefit score estimation through two scoring functions as follows:

(i) Linear scoring model

In this scoring function, instead of minimizing $LW(f)$, we minimized a penalized version as follows:

$$L_W(f) + \lambda\|\beta\|_1 \tag{5}$$

Here, we utilize Least Absolute Shrinkage and Selection Operator (LASSO) [16] penalties and applied it to β for regularization dealing with high dimensionality. Since we are dealing with binary outcome, *Poisson loss* was utilized which can be expressed as:

$$M(y, v) = \left\{yv - e^{-v})\right\} + \lambda\|\beta\|_1 \tag{6}$$

(i) Non-Linear scoring model

In the second scoring function, an additive model represented by $f(X) = \sum_{j=1}^{p} f_j(X_j)$ is utilized. This can be easily accessed by employing the *mgcv* package, which offers comprehensive estimation methodologies tailored for generalized additive models (GAMs). We utilized *logistic loss* also known as *cross-entropy loss* which can be expressed as follows:

$$M(y, v) = \left\{yv - log\left(1 + e^{-v}\right)\right\} \tag{7}$$

3   Results

3.1   Subgroup Identification in MDACC and Mayo Cohort

We compare treatment effects between ICI-Chemo ($T = 1$) and ICI-Mono ($T = 0$) using two scoring methods. Table 1 presents the subgroup and overall treatment effect in MDACC (training) cohort and Mayo Clinic (validation) cohort. The numbers reported in each subgroup, i.e. Recommended ICI-Mono/Received ICI-Mono (16.7%, n = 36) represent the number of patients who suffered early progression both in percentage and count. In the context of subgroup effects, when patients were treated according to system's recommendation, we observed that non-linear scoring system had superior risk reduction in both treatment arms in comparison to linear scoring method (-10.9% to -31.2%) vs. ($+5.6\%$ to -17.2%) in the training cohort. Notice that linear scoring had an increased risk in the ICI-Mono arm. Similarly, in the validation cohort, despite the high percentage of reduction observed in ICI-Mono (-68.9%), the number of samples were significantly skewed. This is evidently shown in the overall effects between linear and non-linear scoring methods in both training (-15.5% vs. $+ -25.4\%$) and validation cohort (-9.6% vs. -14.35). We hence concluded that though linear scoring method shown great risk reduction in the subgroup effects in testing cohort, the skewed number of samples also played a vital role in the overall performance and thus is underperformed in comparison to the non-linear model.

Table 1. (A) MDACC cohort, (B) Mayo cohort. Subgroup effects represent early progression risk reduction when subgroups of patients follow or against recommendation. Overall effect is the weighted average of subgroup effects.

(A) Linear Scoring Model		
Treatments	**Recommended ICI-Mono**	**Recommended ICI-Chemo**
Received ICI-Mono	16.7% ($n = 36$)	32.0% ($n = 128$)
Received ICI-Chemo	11.1% ($n = 9$)	14.8% ($n = 155$)
Subgroup effects	$+ 5.6\%$ ($n = 45$)	-17.2% ($n = 283$)
Overall effects	-15.5%	
Non-Linear Scoring Model		
Treatments	**Recommended ICI-Mono**	**Recommended ICI-Chemo**
Received ICI-Mono	10.7% ($n = 75$)	43.8% ($n = 89$)
Received ICI-Chemo	21.6% ($n = 37$)	12.6% ($n = 127$)
Subgroup effects	-10.9% ($n = 112$)	-31.2% ($n = 216$)
Overall effects	-25.4%	
(B) Linear Scoring Model		
Treatments	**Recommended ICI-Mono**	**Recommended ICI-Chemo**
Received ICI-Mono	31.1% ($n = 3$)	31.3% ($n = 35$)
Received ICI-Chemo	100% ($n = 1$)	22.6% ($n = 41$)
Subgroup effects	-68.9% ($n = 4$)	-8.7% ($n = 76$)
Overall effects	-9.6%	
Non-Linear Scoring Model		
Treatments	**Recommended ICI-Mono**	**Recommended ICI-Chemo**
Received ICI-Mono	31.9% ($n = 11$)	31.0% ($n = 27$)
Received ICI-Chemo	45.8% ($n = 12$)	16.8% ($n = 30$)
Subgroup effects	-13.9% ($n = 23$)	-31.2% ($n = 57$)
Overall effects	-14.3%	

Figure 2 demonstrates the interaction plots for both scoring models. These plots represent the average treatment outcome (weighted risk reduction) within each subgroup

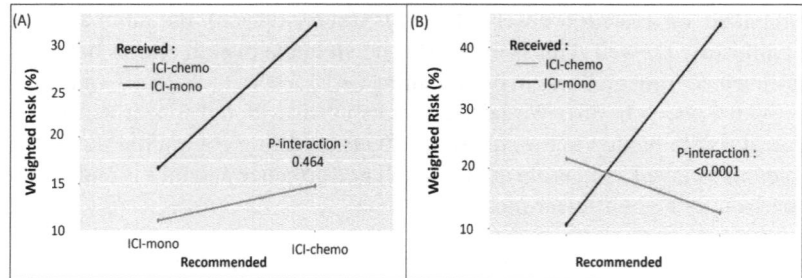

Fig. 2. Interaction plots for (A): Linear scoring system, (B) Non-linear scoring system. All p-values are adjusted using BH method.

broken down by treatment status. If the lines of the interaction plot cross, it indicates there exist a substantial treatment effect. We observed no cross in the linear model (p-interaction = 0.464) but there the lines were crossed in the non-linear model where p-interaction was indeed significant (<0.001).

3.2 Model Interpretation

We further attributed the contribution of individual feature importance to the prediction of the best model (non-linear scoring method) by computing SHAP values to establish the association between each feature and the benefit scores. Figure 3 elucidates the top 12 treatment-moderators that were associated with each treatment arm which were ranked by their magnitude of effect. It was observed that tobacco exposure, lung adenocarcinoma and TP-53 mutated gene were among the top contenders that favors ICI-monotherapy. On the other hand, stage-IVB, KRAS and EGFR mutation had great effect with ICI-chemotherapy.

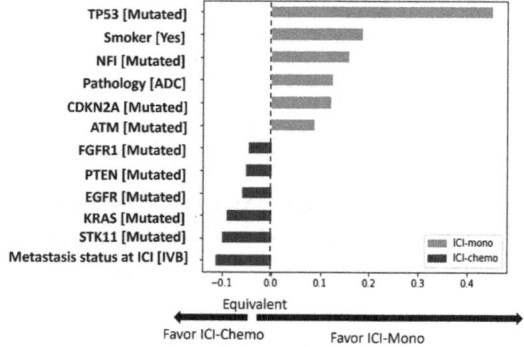

Fig. 3. Treatment moderators associated with efficacy of ICI-mono and ICI-chemo in non-linear scoring model. Horizontal axis represents the effect magnitude.

4 Discussion

In this study, we have investigated optimal treatment selection modeling for NSCLC patients between ICI-Chemo and ICI-Mono using a novel statistical methodology called weighting subgroup identification through formulation of personalized treatment scores. Utilizing a multi-center cohort of 408 patients, we implemented a rigorous three-stage process—propensity score calculation, subgroup estimation, and validation—to effectively categorize patients into appropriate treatment groups. Our approach individualized interventions based on patient-specific characteristics, focusing on those prone to early progression. Unlike models that develop prognostic biomarkers to predict clinical outcomes [17–20], we delve into the realm of predictive biomarkers by leveraging statistical concepts to identify clinico-genomic patterns associated with the benefits of adding chemotherapy to immunotherapy. Using SHAP analysis, we interpreted the model decision and its relationship with individual features, identifying stage-IVB, KRAS, and EGFR mutations as potential beneficial factors in combined immunotherapy. However, the biological relationship between genomic anomalies and immune checkpoint blockade remains complex and evolving. Future research could explore imaging-based avenues and transition from standalone scoring to a composite scoring system.

In summary, we have created and validated a treatment selection model designed to guide individualized immunotherapy, enhancing the efficacy of ICI in late-stage NSCLC by identifying patient subgroups that could benefit from combined immunotherapy and chemotherapy.

References

1. Gabriel, S.E., Normand, S.L.T.: Getting the methods right—the foundation of patient-centered outcomes research. N. Engl. J. Med. **367**(9), 787–790 (2012)
2. Topalian, S.L., Hodi, F.S., Brahmer, J.R., BGettinger, S.N., et al.: Safety, activity, and immune correlates of anti–PD-1 antibody in cancer. N. Engl. J. Med. **366**(26), 2443–2454 (2012)
3. Hong, L., Aminu. M., Li, S., et al.: Efficacy and clinicogenomic correlates of response to immune checkpoint inhibitors alone or with chemotherapy in non-small cell lung cancer. Nat. Commun. **14**(1), 695 (2023)
4. Huling, J.D., Yu, M.: Subgroup identification using the personalized package. J. Stat. Softw. **98**, 1–60 (2018)
5. Su, X., Tsai, C.L., Wang, H., Nickerson, D.M., Li, B.: Subgroup analysis via recursive partitioning. J. Mach. Learn. Res. **10**(2) (2009)
6. Lipkovich, I., Dmitrienko, A., Denne, J., Enas, G.: Subgroup identification based on differential effect search—a recursive partitioning method for establishing response to treatment in patient subpopulations. Stat. Med. **30**(21), 2601–2621 (2011)
7. Foster, J.C., Taylor, J.M., Ruberg, S.J.: Subgroup identification from randomized clinical trial data. Stat. Med. **30**(24), 2867–2880 (2011)
8. Imai, K., Ratkovic, M.: Estimating treatment effect heterogeneity in randomized program evaluation. Ann. Appl. Stat. (2013)
9. Huang, X., et al.: Patient subgroup identification for clinical drug development. Stat. Med. **36**(9), 1414–1428 (2017)
10. Sechidis, K., Papangelou, K., Metcalfe, P.D., Svensson, D., Weatherall, J., Brown, G.: Distinguishing prognostic and predictive biomarkers: an information theoretic approach. Bioinformatics **34**(19), 3365–3376 (2018)

11. Ballarini, N.M., Thomas, M., Rosenkranz, G.K., Bornkamp, B.: Subtee: an R package for subgroup treatment effect estimation in clinical trials. J. Stat. Softw. **99**, 1–17 (2021)
12. Rubin, D.B.: Causal inference using potential outcomes: design, modeling, decisions. J. Am. Stat. Assoc. **100**(469), 322–331 (2005)
13. Al-Tashi, Q., Saad, M.B., Muneer, A., Qureshi, R., et al.: Machine learning models for the identification of prognostic and predictive cancer biomarkers: a systematic review. Int. J. Mol. Sci. **24**(9), 7781 (2023)
14. Ma, J., et al.: A genetic predictive model for precision treatment of diffuse large B-cell lymphoma with early progression. Biomark. Res. **8**, 1–11 (2020)
15. Chen, S., Tian, L., Cai, T., Yu, M.: A general statistical framework for subgroup identification and comparative treatment scoring. Biometrics **73**(4), 1199–1209 (2017)
16. Tibshirani, R.: Regression shrinkage and selection via the lasso. J. R. Stat. Soc. Ser. B Stat Methodol. **58**(1), 267–288 (1996)
17. Saad, M.B., et al.: Predicting benefit from immune checkpoint inhibitors in patients with non-small-cell lung cancer by CT-based ensemble deep learning: a retrospective study. Lancet Digit. Health **5**(7), e404–e420 (2023)
18. Ho, E., et al.: A clinicogenomic model including GARD predicts outcome for radiation treated patients with HPV+ oropharyngeal squamous cell carcinoma. medRxiv (2023)
19. Hoang, T., Dahlberg, S.E., Sandler, A.B., Brahmer, J.R., Schiller, J.H., Johnson, D.H.: Prognostic models to predict survival in non–small-cell lung cancer patients treated with first-line paclitaxel and carboplatin with or without bevacizumab. J. Thorac. Oncol. **7**(9), 1361–1368 (2012)
20. Al-Tashi, Q., et al.: SwarmDeepSurv: swarm intelligence advances deep survival network for prognostic radiomics signatures in four solid cancers. Patterns **4**(8) (2023)

Beyond Conventional Parametric Modeling: Data-Driven Framework for Estimation and Prediction of Time Activity Curves in Dynamic PET Imaging

Niloufar Zakariaei[1,2]([✉]), Arman Rahmim[1,2,3,4], and Eldad Haber[5]

[1] School of Biomedical Engineering, University of British Columbia, Okanagan, Canada
nilouzk@student.ubc.ca, Arman.rahmim@ubc.ca
[2] Department of Integrative Oncology, BC Cancer Research Institute, Vancouver, Canada
[3] Department of Radiology, University of British Columbia, Okanagan, Canada
[4] Department of Physics, University of British Columbia, Okanagan, Canada
[5] Department of Department of Earth, Ocean and Atmospheric Sciences, University of British Columbia, Okanagan, Canada
ehaber@eoas.ubc.ca

Abstract. Dynamic Positron Emission Tomography (dPET) imaging and Time-Activity Curve (TAC) analyses are essential for understanding and quantifying the biodistribution of radiopharmaceuticals over time and space. Traditional compartmental modeling, while foundational, commonly struggles to fully capture the complexities of biological systems, including non-linear dynamics and variability. This study introduces an innovative data-driven neural network-based framework, inspired by Reaction Diffusion systems, designed to address these limitations. Our approach, which adaptively fits TACs from dPET, enables the direct calibration of diffusion coefficients and reaction terms from observed data, offering significant improvements in predictive accuracy and robustness over traditional methods, especially in complex biological scenarios. By more accurately modeling the spatio-temporal dynamics of radiopharmaceuticals, our method advances modeling of pharmacokinetic and pharmacodynamic processes, enabling new possibilities in quantitative nuclear medicine.

Keywords: Dynamic PET · Reaction-Diffusion Neural Network · Predictive Modeling

1 Introduction

Positron Emission Tomography (PET) is a medical imaging technique that uses radioactive pharmaceuticals to visualize and measure body physiological processes, widely applied in oncology, neurology, and cardiology [12,32,34]. Dynamic

© The Author(s), under exclusive license to Springer Nature Switzerland AG 2025
J. Wu et al. (Eds.): CMMCA 2024, LNCS 15181, pp. 99–109, 2025.
https://doi.org/10.1007/978-3-031-73360-4_11

PET, through sequential imaging, allows for the detailed visualization and quantification of radiopharmaceutical distribution within the body over time, providing valuable insights into physiological processes such as blood flow, glucose metabolism, and receptor binding [23].

The processing of dynamic PET data involves image reconstruction followed by generation and analysis of Time-Activity Curves (TACs). TACs are generated by plotting the radioactivity concentration over time in specific regions of interest (ROI) [28]. Subsequently, pharmacokinetic modeling is used to estimate physiological parameters related to the radiopharmaceutical's behavior. Commonly, *parametric models* are used. Such models are based on compartmental modeling, incorporating different physiological compartments and their interconnections. These models are dubbed as parametric models because they contain a small number of parameters (typically less than 10) that govern the shape of the TAC [7,9].

In principle, a reasonable parametric pharmacokinetic model should fit a TAC and be flexible enough to accommodate different TACs from different regions and patients. In particular, Two-Tissue Compartment Model (2TCM) and Three-Tissue Compartment Model (3TCM) are common in practice [9,34]. Since such models contain only a few parameters, they are straightforward to use in order to explain dynamics. However, these models rely on strong assumptions that may not hold under complex biological conditions, potentially limiting their applicability in realistic settings [8,14]. For instance, these models assume it is possible to homogenize each compartment to a constant rate of exchange between compartments, neglecting the variability and non-linear dynamics characteristic of biological systems. Furthermore, these models do not commonly consider the impact of physiological changes in the course of imaging or the influence of underlying pathologies that may alter radiopharmaceutical kinetics and distribution, which can lead to inaccuracies in PET signal interpretation [1,19,31]. There are also issues of patient and/or organ movements over time that may not be fully compensated even with motion correction methods, impacting kinetic models [17]. Finally, research in fields such as emergence [6] suggests that combining even simple properties (like the decay at each cell) can yield a much more complex behavior of the homogenized system.

These limitations highlight the need to extend or refine compartmental models to better capture the complexity of biological systems and enhance PET analysis reliability. A motivating example for this is demonstrated in Fig. 1 where 1 slice of a liver are given at different times.

While some decay is evident initially, it is challenging to justify a specific parametric form. Moreover, averaging across the entire organ yields a curve (see Fig. 2) that does not exhibit typical compartment behavior of single- or multi-exponential biological decay. Observation of the data reveals spatial patterns that are that are not resolved by averaging activity over the organ. These patterns suggest variability in liver function, which could be insightful for therapeutic treatments.

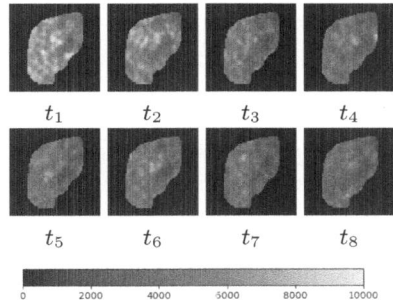

t_1 t_2 t_3 t_4

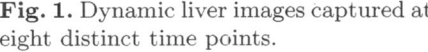

t_5 t_6 t_7 t_8

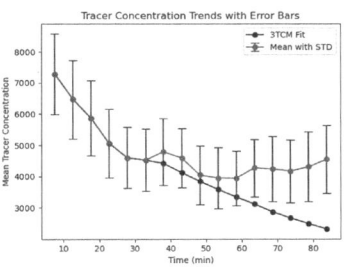

Fig. 1. Dynamic liver images captured at eight distinct time points.

Fig. 2. The average of the TAC curve over the liver, along with its standard deviation. Data is fitted using a three-tissue compartment model (3TCM) based on the early 6 time frames.

The goal of this paper is to propose a **data-driven** methodology for the estimation of TACs, that vary both temporally and spatially. Instead of using a particular parametric form for a TAC, we utilize a carefully designed neural network architecture that aligns with the physical behavior of the phenomena we observe, calibrating its parameters based on the data at hand. Neural network models, far more complex than simple compartmental models, are justified only by their enhanced predictive power. In this work, we show that indeed, these models outperform simple compartmental models, at least for the datasets we have tested.

Neural network architectures that mimic physical systems are now common in many fields of science and engineering [11,13,24]. Such architectures, based on Partial Differential Equations in high dimensions, can be tailored to different physical phenomena, contrasting with compartmental models based on fitting very few parameters in an Ordinary Differential Equations. As highlighted in the literature [11], this approach allows for more tailored and nuanced simulations of physical systems, offering potential advantages over compartmental models in terms of both precision and applicability. Here, we choose an architecture based on a Reaction Diffusion system. The data is used to learn the diffusion coefficients and the reaction term. We show that such a network can fit spatio-temporal patterns observed in the data, obtaining stronger predictive power than classical parametric models. These models can be effectively trained, uncovering new patterns in the data that simple parametric models cannot resolve. Moreover, by using a physically motivated neural network architecture, our network can be seen as an extension of a compartment model into high dimensions.

2   Deriving a Reaction Diffusion Neural Network for the Modeling of TACs

Reaction Diffusion systems have been used extensively in biology [16, 20, 27], from modeling the propagation of electromagnetic waves in the heart [22] to patterns generated on butterfly wings [16]. The equations describe the interaction between a number of species (that can be chemicals or different populations) and their spatial dynamics.

Hinted by its name, the equation comprises two parts: reaction and diffusion. The reaction term is local, meaning it is pointwise. Compartment models can, in fact, be considered as local reaction terms. The diffusion represents the spatial dynamics. Typically, different species have different diffusion coefficients. The interaction between the diffusion and reaction terms is the cause of pattern formation (see the classical work by Turing [33] and references within). The reaction-diffusion equation can be written as

$$\frac{\partial \mathbf{u}}{\partial t} = \kappa \Delta \mathbf{u} + R(\mathbf{u}, t; \boldsymbol{\theta}) \tag{1}$$

with appropriate initial and boundary conditions. Here, $\mathbf{u} = [\mathbf{u}_1, \ldots, \mathbf{u}_c]$ is a vector representing c different species (or in the context of deep networks, channels), and the coefficients $\boldsymbol{\kappa} = [\boldsymbol{\kappa}_1, \ldots, \boldsymbol{\kappa}_s]$ are the diffusion coefficients for each species. The reaction term $R(\mathbf{u}, t; \boldsymbol{\theta})$ couples the different species through nonlinear interaction. Finally, the parameters $\boldsymbol{\theta}$ are trainable parameters in the reaction term.

While reaction diffusion systems have been applied to physical and biological systems for a long time, recent developments in neural network technology have demonstrated that it is possible to derive a neural network interpreted as a reaction diffusion system in high dimensions [24]. In the context of dynamic PET, the image under consideration can be thought of as a weighted sum of different species. In the 2 or 3 compartment model, only 2 or 3 species are used; however, with a deep network, one can employ an arbitrarily large number of species and learn the reaction term, that is, the interaction between them.

Let $I(t, \mathbf{x})$ represent the PET image we aim to model, where both $\mathbf{x}$ and t are discretizations of space and time. Initially, the network embeds $I(\mathbf{x}, t)$ into a higher-dimensional state using a so-called Multilayer Preceptron (MLP) [18]. Let $\mathbf{u}(\mathbf{x}, t) = [\mathbf{u}_1(\mathbf{x}, t), \ldots, \mathbf{u}_c(\mathbf{x}, t)]$ be the embedded state. We assume $\mathbf{u}$ adheres to the reaction diffusion (1) and discretize it in space-time. A common approach for the discretization of such a system is the Implicit-Explicit method (IMEX) (see [2, 3, 25, 26] and references within). Let $\mathbf{A}$ be a discretization of the negative Laplacian. Then the discretization of the system reads

$$\tilde{\mathbf{u}}_{k+1} - \mathbf{u}_k = -h\kappa \mathbf{A} \mathbf{u}_{k+1} \quad \text{and} \quad \mathbf{u}_{k+1} - \tilde{\mathbf{u}}_{k+1} = hR(\tilde{\mathbf{u}}_{k+1}, t; \boldsymbol{\theta}) \tag{2}$$

where h is the time step. The first equation is implicit and requires the solution of the system

$$(\mathbf{I} + h\kappa\mathbf{A})\tilde{\mathbf{u}}_{k+1} = \mathbf{u}_k \tag{3}$$

The solution of a linear system is, in general, slow. However, since the image is defined on a regular grid, the inversion of the method can be efficiently achieved in order $n\log(n)$ (where n is the number of pixels) by using a cosine transform [21]. The reaction term (2) is modeled by a two-layer MLP with the form

$$R(\mathbf{u}, t) = \mathbf{K}_2\sigma(\mathbf{K}_1\mathbf{u} + \mathbf{t}_e). \tag{4}$$

Here, $\mathbf{K}_1$ and $\mathbf{K}_2$ are so-called 1×1 convolutions; i.e., they only mix the channels of $\mathbf{u}$. The function σ is an activation function (here we have used the silu activation) and $\mathbf{t}_e$ is an embedding of the time. Here, similar to diffusion-based methods [30], we have used an MLP

$$\mathbf{t}_e = \mathbf{W}\sigma(t\mathbf{b}) \tag{5}$$

where t is the scalar input time and $\mathbf{b}$ and $\mathbf{W}$ are learnable parameters.

The output of the network is an image: therefore, the network has one final so-called closing layer that compresses the output of the reaction diffusion discretization into a single channel. A sketch of our network is plotted in Fig. 3. Given the time-dependent data, our network learns the MLP that embeds the image, the diffusion coefficients κ, the convolution matrices $\mathbf{K}_1$, $\mathbf{K}_2$, and the time embeddings $\mathbf{b}$ and $\mathbf{W}$. Finally, the network learns the closing MLP layer.

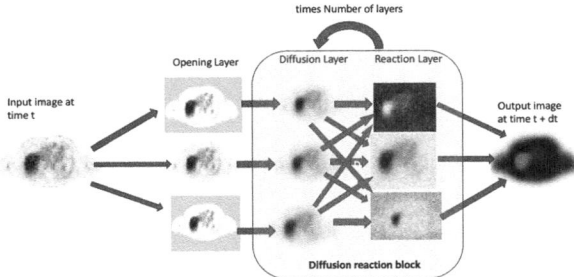

Fig. 3. The reaction diffusion network architecture: An opening layer takes the input image into a higher embedded dimension, where a reaction diffusion network with learned diffusivity and reaction operates. In the example above, 3 channels are utilized to open the image.

Note that similar to Long short-term memory (LSTM's) our network shares parameters between different time steps [29] and also unlike LSTM our network uses time embedding, which makes the function explicitly depend on time. We observed that this allows us to better predict the time behaviour of the system.

3   Training the Network and Dataset

As stated in the introduction, a neural network model can be justified to use if it yields better predictions. Our training process is geared to demonstrate that. Let $I(t_j,\mathbf{x}), j = 1,\ldots,N$ be a set of images obtained from a single patient. For shorthand we define $\mathbf{I}_j = I(t_j,\mathbf{x})$. To this end, we have divided the data set into two groups: a training group $\mathbf{I}_1,\ldots,\mathbf{I}_s$ and a validation set $\mathbf{I}_{s+1},\ldots,\mathbf{I}_N$. Our goal is to train on the training images, in times $t_1,\ldots,t_s$ and for the network to predict the later images that are in the validation set. In the training, we assume to have an image $\mathbf{I}_j$ and we attempt to predict $\mathbf{I}_{j+1}$, that is,

$$\mathbf{I}_{j+1}^{\mathrm{pred}} = f(\mathbf{I}_j, \boldsymbol{\theta}) \tag{6}$$

where $f(\cdot,\cdot)$ is the neural network described above and $\boldsymbol{\theta}$ are the neural network parameters. To calibrate the parameters we minimize the standard Mean Squared Error (MSE) loss $\frac{1}{2}\sum_j \|\mathbf{I}_{j+1}^{\mathrm{pred}}(\boldsymbol{\theta}) - \mathbf{I}_{j+1}\|^2$. The training method is commonly used for LSTM networks [4] and has also been recently proposed for training reaction diffusion networks in the context of graph neural networks [10].

For the minimization process, we utilize the Adam optimizer [15], employing gradient clipping to ensuring the stability. To test the predictability of our model, our network is trained only on the first s time steps, and then it is used to predict the subsequent activity. As mentioned in the introduction, the justification for using a complex model such as a neural network is its ability to predict the TAC beyond its training point, which is crucial for validation. As demonstrated in the following section, our model successfully achieves this objective.

Our research employs a dataset from 7 male patients undergoing [18F]DCFPyL imaging for prostate cancer. The collected data reveal an average age of 70.29 ± 1.89 years, a mean weight of 93.71 ± 18.20 kg and an average administered dose of 7.08 ± 1.31 mCi.

4   Numerical Results and Evaluation

As outlined in Sect. 3, we used the early time frames (here the first 11 frames) of our dataset to train our network to predict the latest frames (last 4 frames). Similarly, we applied this method to the conventional 3TCM using non-linear least squares analysis. Finally, we compared the reaction diffusion network's performance against the conventional 3TCM, benchmarking both against ground truth. Figure 4 clearly illustrates that the reaction diffusion network aligns more closely with the actual data than the 3TCM in the latter four time frames.

The superiority of our model is further evidenced in Fig. 5, which provides a detailed examination of small, defined regions within each organ (15–30 pixels), as detailed in Table 1 and Table 2. Here, we show the result for 3 patients as an example. The neural network's predicted TACs are shown to more accurately reflect the ground truth compared to those produced by 3TCM, which is less accurate when the data doesn't follow a decaying pattern.

The efficacy of our model is quantitatively substantiated in Table 1 and Table 2, which uses the MSE metric, calculated over the test time frames, highlighting our model's predictive strength for future time points. For a robust analysis, five characteristic slices of the targeted organ from each patient were analyzed, aligning with the test time frames.

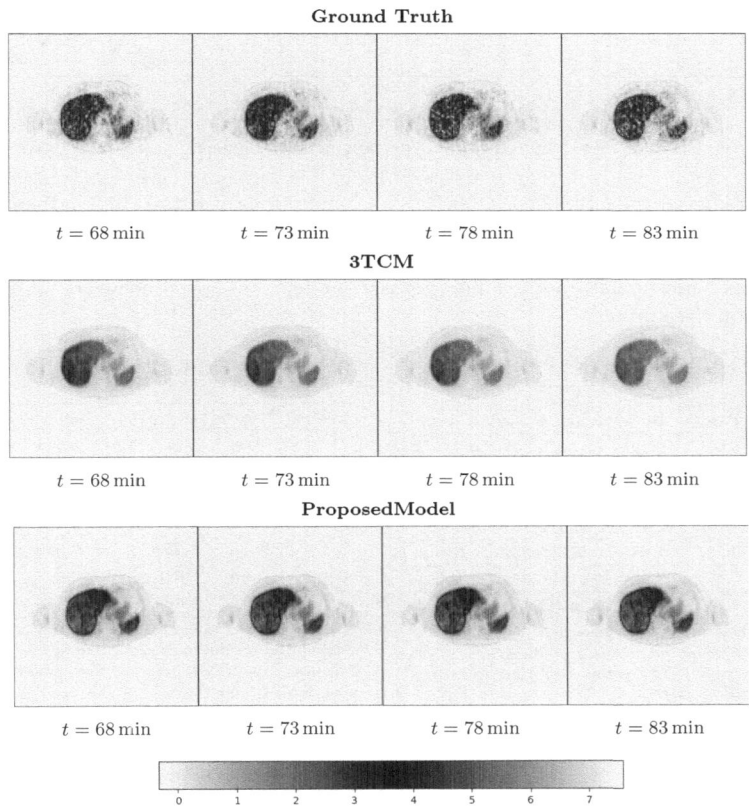

Fig. 4. A selected slice of one of the patients, showcasing the latest time points predicted by our proposed model versus the 3TCM and the original images.

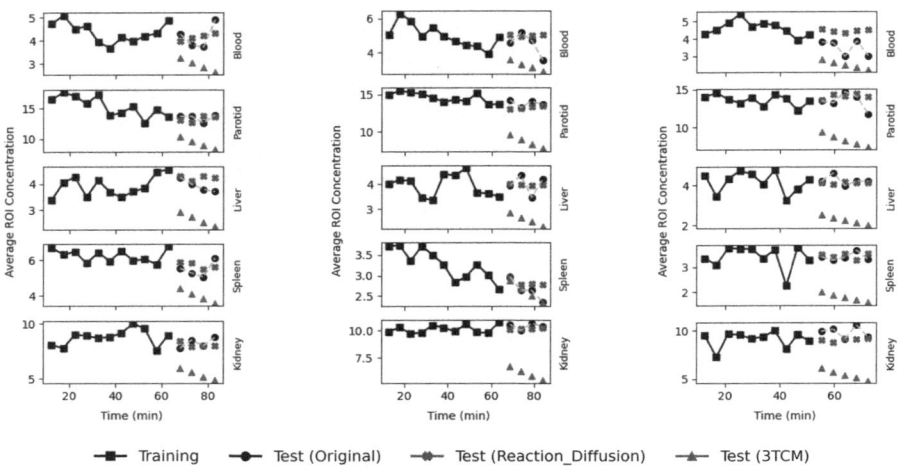

Fig. 5. Predicted vs. actual [^{18}F]DCFPyL concentrations over time in 3 patients. Training data are shown with solid markers, test data with hollow markers. Predictions from the reaction diffusion model and traditional 3TCM are compared with original test. Trend lines connect data points, showing our model's enhanced accuracy in capturing distribution dynamics.

<table>
<tr><td colspan="6">Table 1. Proposed Model</td></tr>
</table>

Patient	Parotid	Blood	Liver	Spleen	Kidney
1	0.685	0.195	0.134	0.207	0.343
2	1.974	0.441	0.115	0.062	0.212
3	0.553	0.665	0.105	0.054	0.121
4	2.752	0.424	0.505	0.151	1.037
5	0.657	1.045	0.687	0.351	1.099
6	1.404	1.085	0.072	0.051	0.942
7	0.750	4.167	0.250	0.189	0.236

Comparison across 5 organs in 7 patients shows the proposed model's predictive accuracy vs. 3TCM over all test time frames, using MSE metric.

Table 2. 3TCM

Patient	Parotid	Blood	Liver	Spleen	Kidney
1	18.08	1.927	1.671	2.611	8.767
2	55.27	1.199	4.701	13.59	17.71
3	27.13	1.822	2.103	0.007	19.05
4	44.63	1.651	3.856	0.715	18.84
5	28.28	0.282	1.661	0.059	2.969
6	27.53	1.076	4.073	2.694	19.60
7	23.36	4.167	3.498	1.758	11.27

Comparison across 5 organs in 7 patients shows the proposed model's predictive accuracy vs. 3TCM over all test time frames, using MSE metric.

5   Discussion and Conclusions

In this paper, we propose the use of a reaction diffusion neural network to model TACs in Dynamic PET imaging. These models replace the commonly used two- and three-compartment models. Although more complex, they offer higher flexibility in fitting data, allowing for better prediction of non-trivial TACs. It is important to note that reaction diffusion neural networks differ from "generic" neural networks and tend to behave similarly to their continuous analogs as extensively used in chemistry and biology [33]. As such, these models can be considered "biological", similar to other reaction diffusion models in biology.

The results obtained by our networks suggest they are far more predictive compared to compartmental models. In fact, our predictions of TACs are superior to any parametric model known to us, suggesting that our model should be considered when a model is needed to predict TAC's. This is particularly meaningful, given the development of complex radiopharmaceuticals (e.g., [^{18}F]DCFPyL and next-gen theranostics) with mechanisms less known than those of older radiopharmaceuticals [5].

One important question remains unanswered: why are reaction diffusion models superior to simpler models that are pointwise (i.e., models that do not include a spatial term)? We hypothesize that the diffusion predicted by the model does not represent only diffusion but also the blurring of the image due to unaccounted-for recovery, motion errors and partial volume effects that leads to blurring which is equivalent to diffusion. The reaction term used in our network is simple, involving only two layers with a single non-linearity. Approximation theory suggests that such an architecture is sufficient to model any continuous function [35]. Thus, while we have presented a data-driven approach to parameter estimation for TACs in dynamic PET, our model's superior predictive power can be both motivated and explainable physically.

References

1. Anderson, R.M., May, R.M.: Infectious Diseases of Humans: Dynamics and Control. Oxford University Press (1991)
2. Ascher, U.: Stabilization of invariants of discretized differential systems. Numerical Algorithms **14**, 1–23 (1997)
3. Ascher, U.: Numerical methods for Evolutionary Differential Equations. SIAM, Philadelphia (2010)
4. Chen, J., Xu, X., Wu, Y., Zheng, H.: GC-LSTM: Graph Convolution Embedded LSTM for Dynamic Link Prediction. arXiv preprint arXiv:1812.04206 (2018)
5. Crişan, G., Moldovean-Cioroianu, N.S., Timaru, D.G., Andrieş, G., Căinap, C., Chiş, V.: Radiopharmaceuticals for pet and spect imaging: a literature review over the last decade. Int. J. Mol. Sci. **23**(9), 5023 (2022)
6. Cucker, F., Smale, S.: On the mathematics of emergence. Japan. J. Math. **2**, 197–227 (2007)
7. De Benetti, F., et al.: Self-supervised learning for physiologically-based pharmacokinetic modeling in dynamic pet. In: Medical Image Computing and Computer Assisted Intervention – MICCAI 2023, pp. 290–299. Springer Nature Switzerland, Cham (2023). https://doi.org/10.1007/978-3-031-43907-0_28
8. Diekmann, O., Heesterbeek, H., Britton, T.: Mathematical Tools for Understanding Infectious Disease Dynamics. Princeton University Press (2012)
9. Dimitrakopoulou-Strauss, A., Pan, L., Sachpekidis, C.: Kinetic modeling and parametric imaging with dynamic pet for oncological applications: general considerations, current clinical applications, and future perspectives. Eur. J. Nucl. Med. Mol. Imaging **48**, 21–39 (2021)
10. Eliasof, M., Haber, E., Treister, E.: Adr-gnn: advection-diffusion-reaction graph neural networks. arXiv preprint arXiv:2307.16092 (2023)

11. Haber, E., Ruthotto, L.: Stable architectures for deep neural networks. arxiv preprint 1705.03341 abs/1705.03341, 1–21 (2017). http://arxiv.org/abs/1705.03341
12. Jadvar, H., Parker, J.: Clinical PET and PET/CT. Springer-Verlag London, 1 edn. (2005). https://doi.org/10.1007/b138777
13. Jin, K.H., McCann, M.T., Froustey, E., Unser, M.: Deep convolutional neural network for inverse problems in imaging. IEEE Trans. Image Process. **26**(9), 4509–4522 (2017)
14. Keeling, M.J., Rohani, P.: Modeling Infectious Diseases in Humans and Animals. Princeton University Press (2008)
15. Kingma, D.P., Ba, J.: Adam: a method for stochastic optimization. arXiv preprint arXiv:1412.6980 (2014)
16. Kondo, S., Miura, T.: Reaction-diffusion model as a framework for understanding biological pattern formation. Science **329**(5999), 1616–1620 (2010)
17. Kotasidis, F.A., Tsoumpas, C., Rahmim, A.: Advanced kinetic modelling strategies: towards adoption in clinical pet imaging. Clin. Trans. Imaging **2**, 219–237 (2014)
18. Krizhevsky, A., Sutskever, I., Hinton, G.: Imagenet classification with deep convolutional neural networks. Adv. Neural. Inf. Process. Syst. **61**, 1097–1105 (2012)
19. Morris, E.D., Endres, C.J., Schmidt, K.C., Christian, B.T., Muzic, R.F., Fisher, R.E.: Kinetic modeling in positron emission tomography. Emission tomography: the fundamentals of PET and SPECT **46**(1), 499–540 (2004)
20. Murray, J.: Parameter space for Turing instability in reaction diffusion mechanisms: a comparison of models. J. Theoretical Biology **98**, 143–162 (1982)
21. Nagy, J., Hansen, P.: Deblurring Images. SIAM, Philadelphia (2006)
22. Panfilov, A., Dierckx, H., Volpert, V.: Reaction-diffusion waves in cardiovascular diseases. Physica D **399**, 1–34 (2019)
23. Rahmim, A., Lodge, M., Karakatsanis, N., et al.: Dynamic whole-body pet imaging: principles, potentials and applications. Eur. J. Nucl. Med. Mol. Imaging **46**, 501–518 (2019)
24. Ruthotto, L., Haber, E.: Deep neural networks motivated by partial differential equations. arXiv preprint arXiv:1804.04272 (2018)
25. Ruuth, S.: Implicit-explicit methods for reaction–diffusion problems. In preparation (1993)
26. Ruuth, S.: Efficient Algorithms for Diffusion-Generated Motion by Mean Curvature. Ph.D. thesis, Institute of Applied Mathematics, University of British Columbia (1996)
27. Schnackenberg, J.: Simple chemical reaction systems with limit cycle behaviour. J. Theoretical Biology **81**, 389–400 (1979)
28. Scipioni, M., Pedemonte, S., Santarelli, M.F., Landini, L.: Probabilistic graphical models for dynamic pet: a novel approach to direct parametric map estimation and image reconstruction. IEEE Trans. Med. Imaging **39**(1), 152–160 (2020). https://doi.org/10.1109/TMI.2019.2922448
29. Seo, Y., Defferrard, M., Vandergheynst, P., Bresson, X.: Structured sequence modeling with graph convolutional recurrent networks. In: Cheng, L., Leung, A.C.S., Ozawa, S. (eds.) ICONIP 2018. LNCS, vol. 11301, pp. 362–373. Springer, Cham (2018). https://doi.org/10.1007/978-3-030-04167-0_33
30. Song, Y., Ermon, S.: Generative modeling by estimating gradients of the data distribution. Advances in Neural Information Processing Systems **32** (2019)
31. Tolles, J., Luong, T.: Modeling epidemics with compartmental models. JAMA **323**(24), 2515–2516 (2020). https://doi.org/10.1001/jama.2020.8420

32. Trotter, J., et al.: Positron emission tomography (pet)/computed tomography (ct) imaging in radiation therapy treatment planning: a review of pet imaging tracers and methods to incorporate pet/ct. Adv. Radiat. Oncol. (2023). https://doi.org/10.1016/j.adro.2023.101212
33. Turing, A.M.: The chemical basis of morphogenesis. Bull. Math. Biol. **52**(1), 153–197 (1990)
34. Wang, G., Rahmim, A., Gunn, R.N.: Pet parametric imaging: past, present, and future. IEEE Trans. Radiation Plasma Med. Sci. **4**(6), 663–675 (2020). https://doi.org/10.1109/TRPMS.2020.3025086
35. Wu, Z., Pan, S., Chen, F., Long, G., Zhang, C., Philip, S.Y.: A comprehensive survey on graph neural networks. IEEE Trans. Neural Networks Learn. Syst. (2020)

Assessment of Radiomics Feature Repeatability and Reproducibility and Their Generalizability Across Image Modalities by Perturbation in Nasopharyngeal Carcinoma Patients

Zongrui Ma[1] , Jiang Zhang[1], Xinzhi Teng[1], Saikit Lam[2], Yuanpeng Zhang[1], Yu-Hua Huang[1], Tian Li[1], Francis Lee[3], and Jing Cai[1(✉)]

[1] Department of Health Technology and Informatics, The Hong Kong Polytechnic University, Hung Hom, Kowloon, Hong Kong SAR
jing.cai@polyu.edu.hk
[2] Department of Biomedical Engineering, The Hong Kong Polytechnic University, Hung Hom, Kowloon, Hong Kong SAR
[3] Department of Clinical Oncology, Queen Elizabeth Hospital, Kings Park, Kowloon, Hong Kong SAR

Abstract. This study aims to evaluate the repeatability and reproducibility of radiomics features (RFs) under image perturbations and examine their generalizability across computed tomography (CT) and magnetic resonance (MR) images among nasopharyngeal carcinoma (NPC) patients. A total of 397 NPC patients with contrast-enhanced computed tomography (CECT), CET1-weight, and T2-weight MR images were analyzed. Image perturbation and contour randomization were implemented to the images and masks to mimic the scanning position and tumor segmentation stochasticity. A total of 1288 RFs from original, Laplacian-of-Gaussian-filtered (LoG) and wavelet-filtered images were extracted. The stability of RF was assessed by adopting median intraclass correlation coefficient (mICC) under patient subsampling. The mean absolute difference (MAD) of the mICC and the accuracy of the binarized repeatability between image datasets were adopted to evaluate its generalizability across image modalities. The MRI-based RFs showed higher stability (77.6% in CET1-w and 80.2% in T2-w with mICC $\geq$ 0.9), whereas the CT-based RFs were less stable (41.7% with mICC $\geq$ 0.9). Overall, 497 RFs (38.6%) had mICC $\geq$ 0.9 in all three modalities. Shape features consistently kept the highest stability in all modalities. MRI-based RFs displayed higher repeatability and reproducibility against scanning position and tumor segmentation variations than CT-based RFs. We urge caution when handling CT-based RFs and advice adopting MRI-based RFs with higher stability during feature pre-selection for stable model construction.

Keywords: Radiomics · Repeatability · Nasopharyngeal Carcinoma

© The Author(s), under exclusive license to Springer Nature Switzerland AG 2025
J. Wu et al. (Eds.): CMMCA 2024, LNCS 15181, pp. 110–119, 2025.
https://doi.org/10.1007/978-3-031-73360-4_12

1 Introduction

Medical imaging is widely used and has an important role in clinical oncology practice. Biomarkers based on medical imaging can be used for screening, staging, intervention planning, and treatment outcome prediction [1–4]. In the current practice of manual evaluation of medical images, radiologists only semantically annotate a small number of clinically significant radiological features. Tumor phenotypes embedded in medical images may contain more information that cannot be easily processed by the naked eyes [3, 5–7]. Radiomics is a computer-based technology for extracting and analyzing quantitative features from medical images. It surpasses the level of details available to the naked eyes and aims to automatically mark clinically significant tumor phenotypes [8].

There are potential pitfalls in radiomics analysis that could jeopardize the generalizability and robustness of established biomarkers. Several approaches have been proposed to reduce the risk of false discovery [9–11]. In particular, repeatability and reproducibility are the first and foremost criteria towards clinical utility. "Repeatability" refers to features that remain the same when imaged multiple times in the same subject. "Reproducibility" refers to features that remain the same when imaged using different equipment, different software, different image acquisition settings, or different processing settings. They should be incorporated into feature pre-selection strategy and downstream predictive model construction in any radiomic studies. On top of that, identifying the stability of radiomics features (RFs) across different image modalities will provide the radiomics community with direct perceptivity for selecting reliable radiomic features and building robust predictive models for implementing precision medicine.

Efforts attempting to bridge this important gap in knowledge have been mainly focused on test-retest experiments [12, 13], which have considerable shortcomings. First, the impact of tumor segmentation variation is often missed in test-retest studies. However, tumor segmentation variability can propagate into significant variability in radiomics feature stability [14, 15]. Two published studies [16, 17] have shown that MR RFs displayed better stability than CT under segmentation variability. Additionally, the limited sample size owing to the need for recruiting consented patients renders their conclusions less statistically convincible. Last but not least, multi-modality and multi-center based RFs stability study is ignored by the limited dataset.

To address these limitations, we attempted to deploy our in-house developed perturbation (image perturbation and contour randomization) framework, taking reference from previous work by Alex et al. [13], to mimic a vast amount of scanning position and tumor segmentation stochasticity via large patient cohorts of nasopharyngeal carcinoma (NPC) patients. Furthermore, we also compared the RF stability under perturbation across three imaging modalities, which is yet to be explored. Accordingly, the objectives of this study are: (i) to ascertain the repeatability and reproducibility of radiomics features via perturbation; and (ii) to examine their generalizability across imaging modalities for NPC patients.

2 Methods and Materials

2.1 Overall Workflow

Figure 1 illustrates the overall study workflow. An internal NPC cohort of 397 patients which consists of contrast-enhanced computed tomography (CECT), contrast-enhanced T1 weighted (CET1-w) MR, and T2 weighted (T2-w) MR were enrolled in this study. Each image modality dataset was processed through preprocessing, image perturbations (rotation and translation), contour randomization and RF extraction before stability evaluation. By comparing the RF stability between each pair of the three imaging modalities, we examined the RFs stability performance disparity across different imaging modalities.

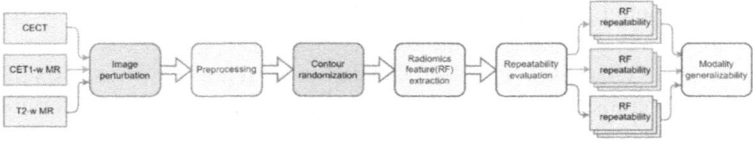

Fig. 1. Overall study workflow

2.2 Patient Cohorts

A total of 397 biopsy-proven (Stage I-IVB) NPC patients who received cancer treatment at the Department of Clinical Oncology of Queen Elizabeth Hospital (QEH) between 2012 and 2016 were retrospectively screened, and 331 patients that had same-institution MR images and eligible target contours were enrolled in the study.

2.3 Image Acquisition and Image Preprocessing

All imaging data were acquired in a Digital Imaging and Communications in Medicine (DICOM) format archived using Picture Archiving and Communication System (PACs). All the calculations were performed by our in-house developed Python-based (3.7.3) pipeline using the SimpleITK (1.2.4) [18] and PyRadiomics (2.2.0) package [19]. The detailed workflow is illustrated in Fig. 1(a). For MR images, the signal intensity was normalized using the brainstem as a reference structure, and N4B bias correction from SimpleITK was employed for MRI inhomogeneity correction.

2.4 Perturbation

We designed the contour randomization as randomized deformation of the original contour. A randomized deformation vector field (DVF) is first generated, followed by normalization and gaussian smoothing controlled by the adjustable kernel size. The deformation field projection on the z-axis is kept constant for the same slice to mimic the slice-by-slice contouring. The final DVF is then scaled by a user-defined factor to control the intensity of the randomization. Finally, the original contour is deformed by the randomized DVF to acquire the randomized contour. The contour randomization will be repeated multiple times, and radiomics features will be extracted from the image masked by the perturbed contours.

2.5 Feature Extraction

Feature computation was performed on the perturbed images using PyRadiomics. Before feature extraction, the perturbed images were preprocessed by isotropic resampling to 1 mm × 1 mm × 1 mm, and the pixel values were shifted by the same offset value of 2000 and further discretized into a fixed bin width of 5. In addition to feature extraction on the original image, Laplacian-of-Gaussian (LoG) filters (Sigma values of 1, 2, 3, 4 and 6 mm) and coilf1 wavelet filters (HHH, HLL, LHL, LLH, LHH, HLH, HHL, LLL) were applied to yield advanced features. The entire set of radiomics features, except shape features, were extracted using the widely used Python package PyRadiomics.

A total of 1288 features were computed for each image. The main groupings of texture analysis features were (1) First-order statistics based on pixel gray-level histograms, 18 features; (2) Shape metrics, 14 features; (3) Statistical features derived from texture matrices including gray-level co-occurrence matrix (GLCM), gray-level size zone matrix (GLSZM), gray-level dependence matrix (GLDM), gray-level run length matrix (GLRLM), neighboring gray tone difference matrix (NGTDM), 73 features (4) Statistical features derived from texture matrices in Laplacian-of-Gaussian (LoG) filtered domain, 455 features; and (5) Statistical features derived from texture matrices in wavelet filtered domains, 728 features.

2.6 Statistical Analysis

Feature stability was quantified using the intraclass correlation coefficient (ICC). Since the perturbation parameters were independently applied to images and masks of different patients, the lower 95% confidence interval of one-way, random, absolute ICC was employed to assess RF repeatability. The calculation was performed by our in-house developed algorithm following the equations presented by McGraw et al. [20]. In our study, median ICC values (mICC) under patient subsampling were adopted as the final metric for assessing RF stability to minimize the potential impacts of outlier patients. Here, an ICC of $\geq 0.75–0.89$ was considered good reproducibility and an ICC ≥ 0.90 was considered excellent reproducibility as recommended by Koo et al. [21].

To compare RFs repeatability performance in different image modalities under contour randomization, we adopted the pairwise Wilcoxon signed-rank test on the ICC value of RFs in each modality. The p-values of the statistical test for all the modalities were tabulated. The tests were one-sided, p-value $<.05$ was considered as significant.

3   Results

One example of random displacement field and randomized contours are shown in Fig. 2. The mean Dice Similarity coefficient and Hausdroff Distance were 0.82 IQR [0.79, 0.85] and 3.2 mm IQR [3, 4.2].

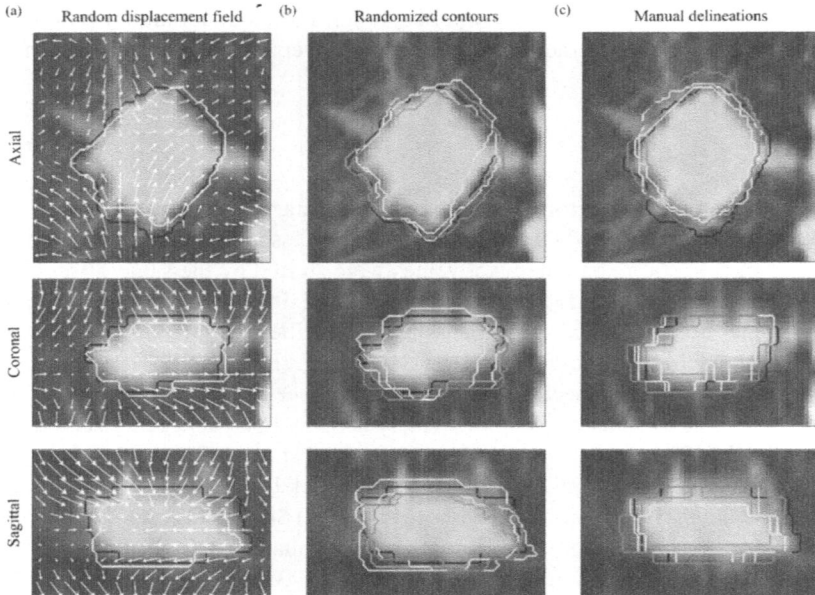

Fig. 2. One example of random displacement field of one slice on the three directions were shown in (a), where the original and the corresponding randomized contour were shown by the red and light green lines respectively. A total of 5 randomized contours in changing colors were superimposed in (b). Similar variations in manuals contours were observed, as shown in (c).

The number of RFs that fell within either the "good" (0.9 > mICC ≥ 0.75) or "excellent" (mICC ≥ 0.9) category for each modality is presented in Table 1. All the shape metrics features fell into the "excellent" category in both CT and MRI. Overall, the CT-based RFs showed the fewest percentage with "excellent" category, 41.7% of all features. This contrasts with the MRI-based RFs from which 77.6% and 80.2% of features had "excellent" stability in CET1-w and T2-w respectively. Across all three imaging modalities, 1069 common features out of the total 1288 features (including all image domains) had a "good" mICC value ≥0.75, and 497 features had an "excellent" mICC value ≥0.9.

First-order and texture features were calculated in 13 image domains: the original image, 5 images with LoG filter with kernel sizes (1, 2, 3, 4, 6 mm), and 8 images from the wavelet decompositions. To explore any variation in feature stability (mICC) by image domains, mICCs for the 18 first-order and 73 texture features were shown by image domain together in Fig. 3. The mICCs from the features for the original image are included in the graph for comparison.

As illustrated in Fig. 4, the CT RFs demonstrated significantly lower mICCs in most LoG-filtered image domains and Wavelet-filtered domains (p-value < 0.01). However, in LoG-filtered domains, the percentage of stable MR RFs decreased from 94% to 77% (T1 > CT) and from 92% to 71% (T2 > CT) when the kernel size changed from 1 mm to 6 mm. Furthermore, the percentage of stable MR RFs ranges from 50% to 99%

Table 1. Number of features(n) and percentage of their groups (%) which fall into "excellent" category (mICC ≥ 0.9) and "good" category (mICC ≥ 0.75) for all features and distinct feature types (first-order, shape, texture, LoG filtered and Wavelet filtered)

	CECT		CET1-w		T2-w	
	n	%	n	%	n	%
All features (1288)						
mICC ≥ 0.9	537	41.7	1000	77.6	1033	80.2
mICC ≥ 0.75	1086	84.3	1235	95.9	1229	95.4
First-order (18)						
mICC ≥ 0.9	10	55.5	17	94.4	18	100
mICC ≥ 0.75	16	88.9	18	100	18	100
Shape Metrix (14)						
mICC ≥ 0.9	14	100	14	100	14	100
mICC ≥ 0.75	14	100	14	100	14	100
Texture (73)						
mICC ≥ 0.9	23	31.5	61	83.5	72	98.6
mICC ≥ 0.75	69	94.5	71	97.3	72	98.6
LoG (455)						
mICC ≥ 0.9	178	39.1	365	80.2	391	85.9
mICC ≥ 0.75	400	87.9	444	97.5	440	96.7
Wavelet (728)						
mICC ≥ 0.9	312	42.9	543	74.6	541	74.3
mICC ≥ 0.75	587	80.6	688	94.5	684	94

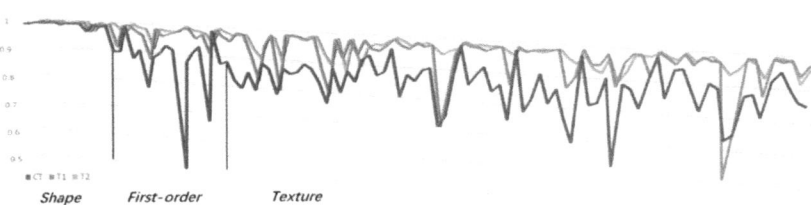

Fig. 3. 3D line chart illustrating the for the shape (n = 14), first-order (n = 18) and texture features (n = 73) derived from original image for CT and MR

(T1 > CT) and from 55% to 97% (T2 > CT) under different wavelet decomposition filters. Especially, the CT and MR RFs exhibited similar stability in LoG-6 mm and Wavelet-HHH domains (p-value > 0.1).

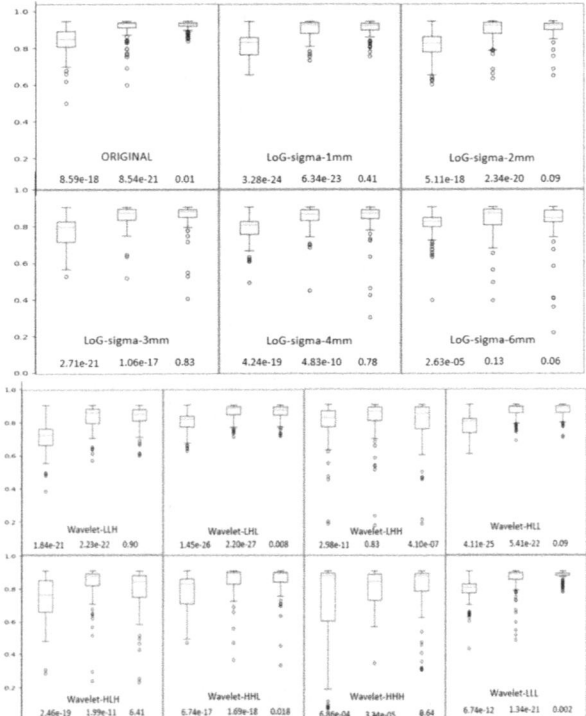

Fig. 4. Boxplots of ICC distribution and p-value between each two modalities on different image modalities and filter categories. In each cell, the three boxplots represent CT, T1 and T2 from left to right. And the p-values below were calculated between CT-T1, CT-T2, T1-T2.

4 Discussion

Radiomics has emerged as a means of image-based prognostication. Ensuring radiomic feature stability is imperative to the external generalizability of downstream predictive models. It is anticipated that this study could provide actionable insights in the selection of stable radiomic features by providing the information of feature repeatability and reproducibility of radiomic features across different imaging modalities. Specially, the two perturbation modes adopted mimicked the variation during image acquisition and tumor segmentation. The image perturbation aims to simulate unavoidable random positional variations during image acquisition. Meanwhile, contour randomization evaluates the random errors derived from manual tumor delineations in clinical scenario.

Three conclusions can be drawn from this study. Firstly, shape features demonstrated the highest repeatability and reproducibility in all modalities. Shape features are generally reported as highly repeatable and reproducible in the literature and were shown to be less sensitive to CT segmentation variation in a phantom study [22]. Further, MRI-based shape features were found to be stable in test-retest of cervical cancer [23, 24]. A recent systematic review, mostly based on CT studies, concluded that shape features showed higher reproducibility than texture features [25].

Secondly, CT-based RFs are more sensitive to scanning position and tumor segmentation variation than MRI-based RFs. The MRI-based RFs were more stable than CT-based RFs. Specifically, the number of repeatable features derived from CT was fewer than the other two modalities. Of the 537 stable features in CT, 92.5% was also stable in the other two modalities. Furthermore, the MRI-based RFs have overwhelming performance when comparing mICC to CT-based RFs with 86.8% and 83.9% RFs with higher mICC from CET1-w and T2-w respectively.

Thirdly, there is no substantial difference in feature stability between the original and filtered image domains. Wavelet and LoG-filtered images showed both better and worse reproducibility than the original images in the three modalities in this study. Similarly, Schwier et al. demonstrated no significant improvement in reproducibility with a certain LoG-filter or wavelet decomposition [26]. On the other hand, Timmeren et al. reported that wavelet features were less reproducible than the unfiltered image features in a test-retest scenario [27]. The number of stable RFs (mICC $\geq$ 0.9) derived from CECT increased from 24 (26.4%) to 55 (60.4%) when the kernel size changed from 1 mm to 6 mm in LoG-filtered image domains whereas this number decreased for MRI-based RFs, 78 (85.7%) to 67 (73.6%) in CET1-w and 81 (89%) to 72 (79.1%) in T2-w.

We acknowledge the limitations in our study. First, our perturbation algorithm may not fully mimic the variation in clinical scenarios owing to technical challenges in fully simulating all the variables. In recent studies, image acquisition, preprocessing, and feature extraction such as image acquisition setting and image reconstruction algorithm were shown to have more significant influence on RFs stability [28]. In addition, the pixel values were discretized into a fixed bin width of 5 in feature extraction, the impact of discretization bin size on feature stability needs to be further explored. Despite the validation of the PyRadiomics platform, results may differ from other radiomic feature extraction platforms. Furthermore, the analysis of deep learning radiomics features stability will be further investigated in the future study. Finally, considering the similar anatomic environment within head and neck cancer, further investigation of other cancer types (e.g., Oropharyngeal cancer) is warranted.

5 Conclusion

Our work is the first study to intentionally scrutinize RF robustness disparity against scanning position and segmentation variations in multi-modality imaging datasets with big sample sizes. In conclusion, CT-based and MRI-based RFs of NPC were evaluated for their repeatability and reproducibility. Shape features emerged as the most stable both in CT and MRI. CT-based RFs displayed higher sensitivity against the scanning position and tumor segmentation stochasticity than MR-based RFs, highlighting the importance of careful feature selection for radiomics generalizability. The feature repeatability results identified by the rather conservative randomizations in this study can be used as the fundamental requirements for building reliable radiomic models in future studies.

References

1. Emaminejad, N., et al.: Fusion of quantitative image and genomic biomarkers to improve prognosis assessment of early stage lung cancer patients. IEEE Trans. Biomed. Eng. **63**, 1034–1043 (2016)
2. Popovici, V., Budinska, E., Dusek, L., Kozubek, M., Bosman, F.: Image-based surrogate biomarkers for molecular subtypes of colorectal cancer. Bioinformatics **33**, 2002–2009 (2017)
3. Scalco, E., Rizzo, G.: Texture analysis of medical images for radiotherapy applications. Br. J. Radiol. **90**, 20160642 (2017)
4. Aerts, H.J., et al.: Decoding tumour phenotype by noninvasive imaging using a quantitative radiomics approach. Nat. Commun.un. **5**, 4006 (2014)
5. Alobaidli, S., Mcquaid, S., South, C., Prakash, V., Evans, P., Nisbet, A.: The role of texture analysis in imaging as an outcome predictor and potential tool in radiotherapy treatment planning. Br. J. Radiol. **87** (2014)
6. Chicklore, S., Goh, V., Siddique, M., Roy, A., Marsden, P.K., Cook, G.J.R.: Quantifying tumour heterogeneity in F-FDG PET/CT imaging by texture analysis. Eur. J. Nucl. Med. Mol. **I**(40), 133–140 (2013)
7. Miles, K.A., Ganeshan, B., Hayball, M.P.: CT texture analysis using the filtration-histogram method: what do the measurements mean? Cancer Imaging **13**, 400–406 (2013)
8. Lambin, P., et al.: Radiomics: extracting more information from medical images using advanced feature analysis. Eur. J. Cancer **48**, 441–446 (2012)
9. Kumar, V., et al.: Radiomics: the process and the challenges. Magn. Reson. Imaging **30**, 1234–1248 (2012)
10. Baumann, K.: Cross-validation as the objective function for variable-selection techniques. Trac-Trend Anal. Chem. **22**, 395–406 (2003)
11. Collins, G.S., Reitsma, J.B., Altman, D.G., Moons, K.G.: Transparent reporting of a multivariable prediction model for individual prognosis or diagnosis (TRIPOD): the TRIPOD statement. Ann. Int. Med. **162**, 55 (2015)
12. Haynes, R.B., McKibbon, K.A., Wilczynski, N.L., Walter, S.D., Werre, S.R., Team, H.: Optimal search strategies for retrieving scientifically strong studies of treatment from medline: analytical survey. BMJ-Br. Med. J. **330**, 1179–1182a (2005)
13. Zwanenburg, A., et al.: Assessing robustness of radiomic features by image perturbation. Sci. Rep. UK **9** (2019)
14. Larue, R.T.H.M., Defraene, G., De Ruysscher, D., Lambin, P., Van Elmpt, W.: Quantitative radiomics studies for tissue characterization: a review of technology and methodological procedures. Br. J. Radiol. **90** (2017)
15. Chalkidou, A., O'Doherty, M.J., Marsden, P.K.: False discovery rates in PET and CT studies with texture features: a systematic review. Plos One **10** (2015)
16. Altman, D.G., Lausen, B., Sauerbrei, W., Schumacher, M.: Dangers of using "optimal" cutpoints in the evaluation of prognostic factors. J. Natl. Cancer Inst. **86**, 829–835 (1994)
17. Bagci, U., Yao, J.H., Miller-Jaster, K., Chen, X.J., Mollura, D.J.: Predicting future morphological changes of lesions from radiotracer uptake in 18F-FDG-PET images. Plos One **8** (2013)
18. Beare, R., Lowekamp, B., Yaniv, Z.: Image segmentation, registration and characterization in R with SimpleITK. J. Stat. Softw. **86**, 1–35 (2018)
19. van Griethuysen, J.J.M., et al.: Computational radiomics system to decode the radiographic phenotype. Cancer Res. **77**, E104–E107 (2017)
20. McGraw, K.O., Wong, S.P.: Forming inferences about some intraclass correlations coefficients. Psychol. Methods **1**, 30 (1996)

21. Koo, T.K., Li, M.Y.: A guideline of selecting and reporting intraclass correlation coefficients for reliability research. J. Chiropr. Med. **15**, 155–163 (2016)
22. Zhao, B., Tan, Y., Tsai, W.Y., Schwartz, L.H., Lu, L.: Exploring variability in CT characterization of tumors: a preliminary phantom study. Transl. Oncol. **7**, 88–93 (2014)
23. Hu, P., et al.: Reproducibility with repeat CT in radiomics study for rectal cancer. Oncotarget **7**, 71440–71446 (2016)
24. Desseroit, M.C., et al.: Reliability of PET/CT shape and heterogeneity features in functional and morphologic components of non-small cell lung cancer tumors: a repeatability analysis in a prospective multicenter cohort. J. Nucl. Med. **58**, 406–411 (2017)
25. Therasse, P., et al.: New guidelines to evaluate the response to treatment in solid tumors. European Organization for Research and Treatment of Cancer, National Cancer Institute of the United States, National Cancer Institute of Canada. J. Nat. Cancer Inst. **92**, 205–216 (2000)
26. Schwier, M., et al.: Repeatability of selected multiparametric prostate MRI radiomics features, arXiv (2018)
27. Zwirewich, C.V., Vedal, S., Miller, R.R., Muller, N.L.: Solitary pulmonary nodule: high-resolution CT and radiologic-pathologic correlation. Radiology **179**, 469–476 (1991)
28. Balagurunathan, Y., et al.: Reproducibility and prognosis of quantitative features extracted from CT images. Transl. Oncol. **7**, 72–87 (2014)

Author Index

© The Editor(s) (if applicable) and The Author(s), under exclusive license
to Springer Nature Switzerland AG 2025
J. Wu et al. (Eds.): CMMCA 2024, LNCS 15181, pp. 121–122, 2025.
https://doi.org/10.1007/978-3-031-73360-4